A winning combination of super strength, courage and ability make TV's Superwomen the most sensational, successful, invincible stars ever to come across a TV screen.

These super heroines use both brains and beauty to combat injustice and villainy worldwide!

TV'S SUPERWOMEN SCRAPBOOK

by SUSAN KATZ

TEMPO BOOKS
GROSSET & DUNLAP, Inc., Publishers, New York, N.Y. 10010
A FILMWAYS COMPANY

TV's Superwomen Scrapbook
Copyright © 1978 by Susan Katz
All rights reserved
Published simultaneously in Canada

ISBN: 0-448-14662-2

A Tempo Books Original
Tempo Books is registered in the U.S. Patent Office
Printed in the United States of America

TV'S SUPERWOMEN SCRAPBOOK

Introduction

Able to leap tall buildings. Check.
Faster than a speeding bullet. Check.
More powerful than a locomotive. Check.

Not a bird. Not a plane. Not even Superman. In fact, not man at all. It's TV's Superwomen, the most watched, most wanted, most glamorous superheroines ever to hit the home screen.

They're an entirely new breed of adventurers who can collectively and individually do *anything* a man could in the name of justice, democracy, and law and order. Two, "Wonder Woman" and "The Bionic Woman," have superhuman powers. "Police Woman" and all of "Charlie's Angels," past and present, use their strength, guts, and instincts.

What they all have is femininity, gorgeous faces, beautiful bodies, a taste for excitement, and a habit of getting into situations fraught with danger and peril.

Wham! Bang! Lynda Carter pirouettes out of uniform and her mousey Diana Prince personality and becomes Wonder Woman, who saves the world from injustice. She is the cavalry to the rescue, all by herself. Angie Dickinson is a beautiful and tough Police Woman: courageous, self-reliant, and good with a gun. And she's not above using her feminine wiles to get her man. As the Bionic Woman, Lindsay Wagner is an electric lady with a pure heart. She'd just as soon use her bionic powers to combat the forces of evil as her wits and beauty, and she never has to worry about breaking a bionic fingernail. Charlie's Angels are the most glamorous, most deadly efficient private eyes in the business. Kate Jackson is one tough lady who relies on her brains more than her beauty. Jackie Smith is the quiet angel with the real street smarts. The newest angel, Cheryl Ladd, doesn't have as much hair as Farrah, but she's eager to please and ready to jump feet first into any rough scrape. And although Farrah Fawcett-Majors may never be an angel again, she is still a superwoman, and as long as she keeps smiling and flashing those teeth in public, she always will be.

They have the world at their feet, their names are household words, and their faces easily the most turned to on the TV dials. They more than just hold their own—they hold their audiences through network changes, format changes, and even cast changes.

They are superwomen by any definition—not just for one hour a week on TV, but all the time, and every place they go!

Chapter 1
Angie Dickinson

Angie Dickinson is one classy lady! Blonde, beautiful, and talented, she may be the oldest of TV's super heroines, but she was also the first.

When NBC found they had a full-fledged smash on their hands in 1974, they had no idea that "Police Woman" was the beginning of the new wave of adventure and action shows starring women. Their heroine was courageous and independent, her job a dangerous one. The hazards of her work were new and exciting to viewers who were getting tired of the same old, familiar plots about male cops. It was new. It was different. And for Angie Dickinson it meant, finally, the kind of recognition and fame she almost had when she first started out—and gave up to get married and have a child.

Having one of the most popular shows on TV— even if it was such a presidential favorite that Gerald Ford used to schedule his news conferences around it—hasn't been all glamour and good times for Angie. As Sgt. Pepper Anderson, Angie takes risks, puts herself into dangerous situations, and proves her courage every week. As Angie Dickinson, she has also taken risks and gotten into dangerous situations—the most visible of them being the seeming end of her 12-year marriage to Academy Award and Emmy winning songwriter/composer Burt Bacharach.

They met in 1963. It was truly something out of a romantic novel. Burt's father, Bert Bacharach, the famous newspaper columnist (Burt's mother, Irma, says that even when she gave birth to her son, the Bacharach's still hadn't decided on a name. They didn't want to make him a junior, so they named him Burt with a "u" to differentiate him from papa Bert with an "e." But his parents always call him "Happy," which he hates), interviewed Angie when she came to New York to promote her latest film, "Captain Newman, M.D." He was immediately taken with the beautiful brown-eyed blonde and did a little matchmaking. Sure that she and his son would make beautiful music together, he gave Burt Angie's phone number.

Burt wasn't quite as enthusiastic as his father. He was recovering from an unsuccessful marriage and was depressed. It took him a year before he got around to calling.

"We met and had the obligatory drink together," as Angie remembers it. "But it was just nothing. Burt disappeared again for six months. Then, to my amazement, he called for another date. This time it was different. When he brought me home

5

that night, I knew this was something very special. We were married two months later." Angie was 33, Burt 37.

The wedding was on May 15, 1965, at 3:30 in the morning in Las Vegas. It was not exactly an auspicious beginning. No honeymoon, just a couple of short hours together and they were off in opposite directions—Burt to London for a concert date, Angie back to the set of "The Chase" and to co-star Marlon Brando. They spent a grand total of nine days together in the first month of their marriage.

They were both trying to get their respective careers moving. Angie was beginning to be recognized as a major talent and was sought after for films and TV. Burt was still waiting for that big break. He had been Vic Damone's accompanist, then Polly Bergen's, the Ames Brothers', and Marlene Dietrich's. The money was okay, but it wasn't what he really wanted to do for the rest of his life. He wanted to write the kind of songs people would remember and sing for years.

When on July 12, 1966, their daughter, Lea Nikki Bacharach, was born, things began to change. The baby was three months premature and only weighed one pound-one ounce. The doctors didn't expect Nikki to live.

Angie and Burt were shattered. There was nothing they could do but hope and pray, and put their complete faith in the doctors. Angie decided then and there that this child was more important than a career, and she more or less retired to give all her care and attention to Nikki.

"Burt and I watched her by the hour," she says. "Whenever she gained an ounce, it was cause for celebration."

The cost of caring for Nikki was astronomical—both financially and emotionally. There were, of course, round-the-clock nurses and specialists. Every possible medical resource was made available. Still, the doctors feared there might be brain damage, possibly even blindness.

"In the hospital, Burt and I just stood there, looking helplessly through a glass window while the doctors fought to save her," remembers Angie. "Her head wasn't even as large as a baseball. Finally, they told us she would live."

It was a blessed relief, and one that sent Burt into a frenzy of musical activity. Work was his way of dealing with the heartbreaking months of Nikki's slow, almost unnoticeable progress. Angie stayed home and spent every waking moment with the baby. It wasn't in any way that Burt was shirking his responsibility as a father and husband. Not at all. He knew that money was needed to pay for the special care the baby was getting, and he knew Angie was worried about it. He and his song-writing partner, Hal David, had one small success with "Magic Moments" just before the baby's birth. Now it was time for the big one. The fates smiled. Dionne Warwick recorded "Do You Know The Way To San Jose" and made it a hit. Then, incredibly, it was nothing but hit after hit. "Alfie," "I'll Never Fall In Love Again," "What The World Needs Now," "Walk On By," the score for the Broadway smash, "Promises, Promises," and, of course, an Academy Award for "Raindrops Keep Fallin' On My Head," and another for the whole score of "Butch Cassidy and the Sundance Kid." He had made it to the top.

Angie was content to stay home with Nikki, who was making steady progress and was a constant joy and wonder to her doting parents. She didn't miss being in front of the cameras. She didn't even mind playing "second fiddle" to Burt, who was so much the golden boy of the hour that Angie was literally elbowed out of the way when they were out together by fans trying to crawl all over him. Not only did they adore his music, but his boyish good looks drove the ladies wild. Actually Angie liked the idea of being married to a man that other women would have liked to come home to. It kept the excitement and mystery in their marriage, even if she did occasionally get an elbow in the ribs from some overzealous admirer of Burt's.

But Angie also didn't want to let her career totally fall by the wayside while she was caring for Nikki and Burt—nor did her husband want her to.

"You're far too good an actress not to use your talents," he told her, trying to convince Angie to go back to work at least part of the time. Not only that, Burt felt it wasn't good for Nikki to have Angie giving that much time to her—she was too overprotective and too permissive with the child.

"Nikki *was* slow to learn, but only slow," Angie says, "not retarded. Now we wish she sometimes wouldn't learn so fast."

Nikki's progress was amazing. She was bright,

pretty, and well-coordinated for her age. Her only real problem was her eyes. She was unable to focus them both on one spot and had already undergone surgery to partially correct the problem. She wore thick glasses most of the time, but the doctors promised Angie and Burt that the situation would clear up as she got older.

"As she was developing into a normal healthy child," her mother recalls, "she was also developing some normal healthy habits, like screaming to get her way and taking advantage of me. So I went back to work."

Going back to work meant making a few terribly undistinguished films like "Pretty Maids All In A Row" with Rock Hudson, "The Resurrection of Zachery Wheeler," and "Second Face." Whether or not Angie accepted a part was partially based on Burt's schedule. She wanted to work, but she was not ready to give up being able to pack up Nikki and fly to England with Burt for a couple of months if that's where he was going. Their time together was very precious, and more important than anything else.

She turned down the role of Hot Lips Houlihan in "M*A*S*H*" because the location shots would take her too far from home for too long. It turned out to be Sally Kellerman's big break. Angie accepted, instead, things that were quick and close.

One of those was the part of Sgt. Suzanne "Pepper" Anderson in "The Gambit," an episode of "Police Story." Critics and viewers alike loved both the show and Angie. Letters and calls poured in to NBC: when was Pepper coming back?

NBC offered Angie a series based on the character of Pepper. She wasn't sure whether to accept the part. It would mean long hours away from her family, and Angie just didn't know if she was ready for that. She dug up every imaginable reason why not to do it.

"I never thought I'd concentrate on television until I was gray-haired, Nikki was in college, and Lucille Ball returned to do a series so I could be cast as her next-door neighbor," Angie laughed. "Television? That's not a career for a human being —at least not for a devoted wife and mother whose first thoughts are for Burt's comfort and happiness and for those of our child."

It was Burt who cajoled and convinced Angie to accept the "Police Woman" offer. It took some doing, but he finally made her believe that she had given up enough for her family. It was time for her to think of her career.

"I felt she deserved the shot at television stardom," Burt said. "I always felt Angie was a first-rate actress, just waiting for the right opportunity, accepting roles that were less than her abilities called for because she wouldn't go on location or leave us for any length of time."

Burt was quite the sympathetic and understanding husband, even though his own career was beginning to level out. He was suffering from a malady that often affects musicians—the fear that his next song would be, literally, a clinker. As if prophetically, he did the score for the cinematic bomb of 1973, "Lost Horizons." Then, his long time association with Hal David came to an abrupt end over the movie version of "Promises, Promises." Twentieth Century-Fox wanted Neil Simon, who wrote the book for the show, to do the screenplay and Neil's wife, Marsha Mason, to star. There were some problems and the production was delayed. It was a difficult time for Burt, but he knew how much Angie needed his support.

Angie really wanted that chance to be a star, to build on the foundations of a promising career that had been inactive too long. Her ego definitely needed that boost up the ladder of success. Besides, Nikki was seven and in school. The break was good for both of them, and Angie didn't have to feel guilty about going back to work. One thing she did insist on, besides a nice $25,000 per episode salary, was a contract that stipulated a four-and-a-half day week, and a daily wrap-up time of 6:00 PM so she could get home, make dinner, and spend some time with her family.

Family has always been important to Angie, beginning with her earliest memories of growing up in Kulm, North Dakota, population 700. She was the third daughter, after Mary Lou and Janet, for the Brown family. Mother and dad owned, edited, and published the *Kulm Messenger*. They worked hard but eventually gave it up and moved to a slightly larger town, Edgely, population 900. Angie (born Angeline Brown) was never interested in newspaper work. It just didn't have the kind of glamour she was looking for. When Angie was nine, the family took off for warmer climes and the sunny skies of Burbank, California. The brutal North Dakota winters were just too difficult for everyone.

Angie went to parochial schools, taking stenography and typing to prepare herself for the world of business. She never dreamed of becoming a movie star: she would get a job, get married, and have children. She tried Immaculate Heart and Glendale Colleges for a while, but academic life just wasn't for her. She did meet, though—and marry—handsome, young campus football hero, Gene Dickinson. It was a mistake: they were both too young, and it didn't work. But Angie was never bitter about it, she just accepted it as something that had to happen. It didn't sour her thinking about marriage either: she always knew she'd make some man a good wife some day; it was only a matter of time. Besides, she now had a last name that was far more appealing than just plain Brown.

Angie had a job in the office of an aircraft company in Burbank. It wasn't terribly glamorous, but she was, and some of her co-workers sent her picture in to a beauty contest. Much to everyone's surprise, she won. The prize was acting lessons with Batami Schneider, the wife of the acting coach at Columbia Pictures. Angie was something less than enthusiastic about the whole thing—she kept right on working at the aircraft company anyway.

But it couldn't and didn't last. Angie was beginning to get noticed. TV job offers started rolling in. The most important one was in the chorus line on "The Jimmy Durante Show." Director Howard

Hawks, who was well-known for having an eye for young and beautiful new actresses—he was the one who cast Lauren Bacall in "To Have And Have Not" opposite Humphrey Bogart, which not only established her professionally but won her a husband as well—caught Angie's beauty on TV and signed her to a personal contract. She was just 26 and about to play her first really important role—Feathers in Hawks' "Rio Bravo." She was the only woman in the film, which starred John Wayne, Dean Martin, and Ricky Nelson.

She was a smash! Of course, her natural beauty and talent had something to do with it. But Hawks also insisted that she be given the full and royal studio publicity treatment. And she was—her name and face were seen everywhere. It paid off. Hawks sold half her contract to Warner Bros., who immediately put her to work in the soap opera-ish "The Bramble Bush," with Richard Burton. Then came "Oceans 11," with Frank Sinatra and his "Rat Pack." Angie and Frank dated for a while, but it was never anything serious. As Angie describes it, "He wasn't the sort of man I could ever live with. But we can still say 'I love you' to each other."

Being a fringe member of the "Rat Pack" had its rewards. One of its charter members was Peter Lawford, brother-in-law of John F. Kennedy. Lawford introduced Angie and Jack, and she became an enthusiastic campaigner and was easily welcomed into the family fold by Ethel, Bobby, and Joan. They spent many hours together on the campaign trail, sharing jokes, stories, and gossip. Angie never did get friendly with Jackie Kennedy, who stayed away from the small parties the Camelot inner circle had. But Angie was solidly in with the rest of the Kennedys, and she was having a fantastic time. It was fun. It was exciting. And Angie had it all—she was single, at the peak of her career, and a favorite of the President of the United States!

"What a style he had," she says of JFK. "What a profile! He really gave this country a shot of get up and go."

It all came to a very tragic end with the assassination of JFK. Angie mourned with the family and the rest of the world; but, eventually, she dried her tears and went on with her life and her career. By the time she met and married Burt, Angie was in constant demand for movies. She made at least half a dozen between 1960 and 1965; but she was able to give it all up for Burt with no regrets—a husband and children had always been what she wanted most. But in 1974 a turning point occurred: the Bacharachs had been married for nine years, and their life together had changed. Burt was a big star, but his career was at a standstill. Their marriage, which Angie had called "blissful and glorious" was having its ups and downs. They had even separated a couple of times because they thought perhaps absence would make the heart grow fonder. They always got back together after a short while, so apparently it worked.

"A lot of people stay together because they

can't afford to split up," Angie says. "But when you stay together even when you *can* afford to live apart, then it must mean something. I'm very much in love, and I know Burt is very much in love. And this can be kind of dumb and risky. It's like a snowball. It gets bigger, maybe better, maybe not better, but it changes form as you go along."

But Angie had just ignored the rumors about Burt's gambling and dating other women. She was working doubly hard in order to keep her marriage together and to make "Police Woman" a success.

With the show, she succeeded beyond her wildest dreams. When it premiered, in September 1974, Angie was anxious. She loved the idea of playing someone who was bad and good at the same time: she had always enjoyed meaty roles, "bad girls or glamorous girls with humor." But this was different from a movie, it was a weekly series, with new challenges every seven days.

The plots on "Police Woman" were grown up and serious, part of the new trend toward realistic cop stories that began with "Police Story." They showed cops as human beings, sometimes good, sometimes rotten.

"The girl I'm playing iş not a Puritan," Angie said about Pepper's character. "She's a free woman in a free world."

The series was intended to be real, not phoney and exploitative. June Lang, the real-life police-woman who supposedly inspired the show and advised scriptwriters and stars about how a woman cop, in particular, deals with given situations, thinks Angie does a fine job as Pepper—that she's believable and real, as are the plots. June, who is now retired from police work and who contributed many plot suggestions based on her own experiences, says, "I'm astonished that Angie has the role down so well—not like those other women cops on TV. What's so great is that she doesn't come off like a pistol packin' momma."

Everyone connected with "Police Woman" was a little concerned about whether the TV public could accept a woman doing what has always been a man's job. Policewomen, in the past, had always been relegated to a desk or a dispatcher's phone—not just on TV but in real life as well—so Angie was enthusiastic about the opportunity.

"It's great to be first with an idea. 'Police Woman' was first in casting a woman in the lead for that kind of dramatic show. Yes, it's great to get there first—unless, of course, it's with an Edsel. To me, it's all natural enough. I don't feel as if I'm playing a man's role—not at all."

The International Conference of Police Chiefs, meeting in Washington, D.C., felt that she was making such an important contribution towards easing the acceptance of actual policewomen into police departments all over the country that they gave her an award. It's one of her most treasured possessions.

Angie feels that as Sgt. Pepper Anderson she finally has the chance to develop a total character. "Maybe there was 20 percent of me in a picture before," says Angie. "I have a sense of humor, glamour, and creativity. Now I can put them all together: I get to be them and do them all, instead of just being attractive and interesting.

"Women have been basically mothers and wives. They're bank tellers and typists and secretaries. You've got to be doing something interesting—there has to be an attraction for an audience—if you're going to put a story on the screen the best thing to do is present it realistically."

It's no wonder Angie's favorite script was the one in which she got to wear lots of wigs and disguises and go out on the street! It wasn't as if she could go back into her past and conjure up memories of daring and excitement in Kulm. They didn't even have a police department. "I played cops and robbers a lot," Angie laughs. "Gary Cooper was my ideal. I always draw from the hip."

Meanwhile, back on the home front, Angie's job was getting in the way of her happy family life.

She and Burt were beginning to have to make appointments to see each other. She was usually out of the house by 6:30 AM to be on the set by 7:00. She had to give up driving Nikki to school, marketing, housekeeping, and her singing and drama lessons. When she got home from work, some 12 hours later, it was for a quick dinner, an hour or two with Nikki, studying her script for the next day, and sleep. When Burt wasn't working, he was playing tennis or tending to the eleven thoroughbred horses he races. It wasn't the best of times for either of them.

When the first season was over, Angie knew she couldn't keep up with that kind of schedule. Her new contract stated that she start work no earlier than 9:00 AM, so she could at least have some additional time with Nikki: they would do their exercises together every morning. "The air is fresh in the morning, and the sky is always blue," Angie explained. "I'm making a point to raise Nikki to be fitness-minded. But our daily routine is mostly for my benefit. Doing a TV series is exhausting work, but there's a lot of time sitting around. It's a great temptation to get physically lazy, eat big lunches, and gain nothing but weight."

No worries, Angie manages to keep at a trim 113 pounds without too much effort. And Nikki is every bit as determined as her mom to stay in shape. She's grown up into a delightful young lady, and both her parents are terribly proud of her. When Angie says she is "remarkable," that's not just a proud mother's voice you hear. It's the voice of a parent truly thankful for her child's life. "She has such intensity with whatever she does." mama gloats. "She plays wonderful piano. In ballet it's the same thing. She always wants to win and win and win, and do so well at anything. Fascinating."

Nikki is twelve now and able to understand about the long hours required to do a TV series. What she can't understand is why mommy and daddy can't stay together anymore.

Angie was having a little difficulty with that herself. When she wrapped up the first season of "Police Woman," she came home totally exhausted. She couldn't wait up for Burt, so she went to bed and left him a note: "The last day! Thank you for your help and your understanding." She tried to sleep, but what she really wanted, even

18

more than rest, was to hear her husband say that it hadn't been all that terrible, her working so hard. He didn't say anything, and Angie interpreted his non-response to mean "it was worse than he expected and he wasn't happy with my being away from home so much."

His unspoken message was, of course, that she was going to have to make a choice, sooner or later, between "Police Woman" and Burt Bacharach. It took a bit more than a year for it to reach the real crisis point, but in September 1976, just as "Police Woman" was about to start its third season, and Burt was about to record a new album and do a series of concert dates, they announced a separation.

How ironic! It had been Burt who urged Angie to get back to work in the first place. Now, it seemed, he was having problems adjusting to her success and her devotion to her career.

They both totally immersed themselves into frenetic work schedules. Burt to New York to record his album and then to Lake Tahoe, Las Vegas, and all over for his live appearances. Angie worked harder than ever on "Police Woman" and spent whatever time there was left with Nikki.

It hasn't been easy for either of them. Angie's certainly not happy that her marriage is over. She needs the kind of satisfaction and fulfillment her career gives her even if it means, at this point, no time for any men in her life.

Burt hasn't exactly had an active social life either; he's still depressed over the split, and he misses his family very much.

They do keep in touch. Burt calls regularly, though Angie no longer sits by the phone waiting for his calls as she did in the beginning. They spent Christmas together, mostly for Nikki's sake, but also because they truly wanted to. Angie flew to Lake Tahoe and spent a weekend with Burt, and close friends hoped that a reconciliation was in the works. But it didn't come about. She also spent some time with him in Las Vegas last fall: they were seen sharing a bottle of vintage wine and looking happy to be together. But nothing more came of that either.

"Police Woman" is in its fourth and last season. It's already been picked up for late night reruns on ABC. Angie's plans for the future are not yet firm, although it's been reported that she and Burt have talked about doing a musical together. Burt would, naturally, write the music, and Angie would sing and dance. (Her only other professional musical appearance was singing "I'll Never Fall In Love Again" with Burt at a charity benefit. "It's really painful competing with Dionne Warwick," Angie joked at the time. "She's so good.") Burt's album, "Futures," is doing well, and he's hoping it will help revive his popularity and his spirits.

You don't just take eleven years of a "perfect marriage" and toss them away like so much used Kleenex—even when its between two show business people whose careers have never managed to be on an upswing or a decline at the same time. It's lonely and difficult for each one and especially heartbreaking when there's an adored child involved.

But, if Burt is now ready and willing to accept Angie's career as not just her right but as a vital and necessary part of her life; and if his own career picks up and restores some of his self-esteem, maybe there's hope. They have separated before and managed to work things out.

Angie's favorite Bacharach tunes are "Don't Make Me Over" and "Make It Easy On Yourself." They're particularly appropriate to the Bacharach's situation as it presently stands.

"But," Angie says, with a rather sad smile, "I loved them even when our love was unshatterable."

Chapter 2
Lynda Carter

Great Hera! Lynda Carter traded in her bathing suit and her Miss World-USA title for a golden breastplate and star-spangled hotpants and became the new Wonder Woman.

Great Hera again! Right out of the pages of Charles Moulton's 1942 comic strip creation came the idea for TV's superest super heroine.

She was immortal, an Amazon who fled from the ancient Greek, male-dominated society of 200 B.C. to Paradise Island, unchartered and undisturbed, at least until a U.S. Army plane, piloted by Major Steve Trevor, crash-landed on the Amazon's utopian acreage.

Wonder Woman—Diana to her close friends— fell madly in love with the Major, whom she nursed back to robust health. Obviously, she couldn't just pick up and leave her fellow Amazonians for a mere mortal. So she took a sort of leave of absence from the island and, disguised as the relatively unattractive Yeoman First Class, Diana Prince, arrives in the United States to be assigned as secretary to Major Trevor. He has absolutely no idea that she and Wonder Woman are one and the same. When circumstances call for saving the United States—and/or Steve—from peril, evil, or what-have-you, Diana Wonder Womanizes herself with a quick twist and slips out of her uniform and into her red, white, and blue finery. Her golden belt gives her the superhuman strength to fight her enemies; the silver cuffs are the perfect accessory for deflecting bullets, and her golden lasso forces whomever she wraps it around to tell nothing but the truth.

The way the series actually came into being is an interesting bit of television politics. Warner Communications, who owns the company that puts out "Wonder Woman Comics," decided that if Universal could get away with its almost-comic strip series—"The Six Million Dollar Man"—they could go one better. They had the real thing.

In 1974, the first "Wonder Woman" pilot, set in the present, hit the airwaves. It starred Cathy Lee Crosby, a fragile blonde, and it didn't work. But in the best traditions of never letting go of a good idea, and with the hope that it might yet be a hit, the producers, Douglas C. Cramer and Bud Baumes, decided to try and capitalize on the nostalgia craze and put the setting back to 1942, "An age of innocence when you could tell the good guys from the bad guys," as Cramer put it. As for a star, they were searching for a "dark-haired girl who *looks* like the girl in the strip. She should be built like a javelin-thrower, but with the sweet face of Mary Tyler Moore."

Enter Lynda Carter. While Cramer, Baumes, and Warner Bros. were knocking themselves out looking for what even they thought was the impossible, Lynda was quietly fulfilling all their requirements—only neither she nor they knew it yet.

Lynda came to Hollywood by way of Arizona and the Miss World Pageant, but it wasn't an altogether painless trip. Along the way were all the frustrations, disappointments, and broken hearts that any 25-year-old beauty could handle.

Growing up in Phoenix was a mixed blessing. Lynda is the youngest of three and just missed out on her family's good years. There was wealth and prosperity just until after she was born; her father was an antiques dealer, though Lynda prefers the more descriptive, "junkman—like Sanford and Son." Whatever you want to call it, antiques or junk, the Carter family suffered from some heavy financial setbacks, especially during Lynda's adolescence. That might have traumatized a lot of young girls, but Lynda was showing her super potential even then.

"I knew I had to go out and work to help out at home," Lynda says, "so that's what I did. I took any job I could get, including working as a maid in other people's homes. I saw nothing wrong in that."

If that didn't make it difficult enough, her high school years at Phoenix' Arcadia High, were not much easier to take. She was, as she says, "Taller than all the boys except the tackles on the football team, and all my girlfriends seemed to be 5'3" blondes. I was even rejected as a pom-pom girl because I towered over everyone else."

Fortunately for Lynda, she channeled her teen-aged disappointments and frustrations in a creative direction by taking singing lessons and writing songs. At 15, she joined a folk group called Just Us and toured with them throughout high school and for three years after graduation. She had enrolled in Arizona State University, but the thought of a singing career seemed much more attractive than a college degree, and she dropped out early on. She was not exactly the singing rage, however, so Lynda ended up back in Phoenix with nothing much else to do but enter a beauty contest.

She won first prize. And why not? She was a gorgeous 5' 10", with a stunning figure, very special blueish-greyish-greenish eyes, and lustrous long dark hair. It was the winning combination. She was clearly the most beautiful woman in the contest. Her next step was to the Miss Arizona-World contest, which she also won, and then Miss World-USA with a fighting chance at the Miss World crown. She didn't win—Miss Australia did—and she was terribly disappointed. But the rewards of being Miss World-USA were plentiful, and Lynda the beautiful reigned for a glorious, public appearance filled year.

It was often a hectic and demanding job—being beautiful, pleasant, smiling, and cooperative all the time—but Lynda has nothing but good things to say about that year and about the phenomenon of beauty contests in general. A lot of people put them down as exploitative, inane, fiercely competitive, and placing emphasis on unimportant values in today's society, but Lynda disagrees.

"I think beauty contests are great," the former Miss World enthuses. "How else can a girl of a moderate income family get a chance to meet all the interesting people and see all the things I did?"

How else indeed? Look where it led her. From Phoenix to London to Hollywood to study acting. A lucky meeting with producers Cramer and Baumes, and Lynda was launched as Wonder Woman on November 7, 1975, on ABC. The ratings for that first show were more than just good, they were quite terrific, but ABC hesitated to commit themselves to positioning the show for the 1976 season. They already had "The Bionic Woman" scheduled as a series, and two superwomen would be one too many, they thought. Prodded by an offer from CBS (a rather prophetic one) to buy the series from Warners, ABC scheduled "Wonder Woman" for two one-hour specials that ran in April. Again, the ratings were better than good, yet ABC still wouldn't come up with a permanent time slot. In stepped NBC, claiming they would buy the series for their fall line-up if ABC didn't do something quick.

ABC did do something quick, and very unusual. They scheduled "Wonder Woman" specials, in different lengths, on a prime-time, pre-emptive basis. It was a new idea in programming that unfortunately didn't work for long. The ratings were good, but fans just couldn't get a grip on the timing. "Wonder Woman" was not on a regular enough basis to build up a really strong and loyal following. So when ABC announced their fall 1977 schedule, "Wonder Woman" (and "The Bionic Woman" as well) were nowhere to be found. ABC's reason? They were overcommitted to new shows, and they felt there was a definite trend toward comedy rather than toward female superwomen type adventures. Just to show how farsighted they were, of the 22 new shows that premiered in September 1977, only two made it through to the new year—"Love Boat" and "Soap," both ABC and both comedies.

Luckily for everyone, CBS came to the rescue, and "Wonder Woman" became safely ensconced in a new home.

They bought the show for 26 regularly scheduled one hour episodes. They were at least partially convinced to do it by Ron Samuels, Lynda's husband, agent, and all-around magic maker. He is the driving force behind many of TV's top money-making stars. CBS switched the format to a modern setting, partially for money reasons, partially to give it more flexibility. As a "period" series, it was expensive, with a lot of dollars being spent on props, costumes, and costly 40's sets. It was also getting boring, fighting all those Nazis, and the new format gives Lynda a little bigger range.

"The plots have been—and will be—based on domestic and international problems," Lynda explains. "Some of the guest leads are 'larger than life' in terms of destructive power, and then other shows will be based on a more human interest slant. The scope is wider—from outer space to a child in trouble, perhaps."

To anyone who missed the first episode, "The Return of Wonder Woman," the total turn-around might have been a bit confusing. In that show, Diana finished up her duties in the United States just after World War II was over and went home to Paradise Island. Then, another plane crashed, and another Steve Trevor survived—but this time, it's the original major's son (remember, Wonder Woman is immortal and ageless), played once again by Lyle Waggoner. And so, life and Wonder Woman continue on. . . .

As for Lynda, she's as unlike Wonder Woman offstage as you could possibly imagine. She's had a tough job with the character, who has enjoyed a comic strip existence for more than 25 years. The original "Wonder Woman" cartoon was created because Charles Moulton felt little girls were being left out. The boys had "Superman," "Batman," and "Captain Marvel" to follow in the funny papers, but there were no superwomen. So he invented one. And thousands of young girls grew up with the fantasy of someday changing their own hum-drum lives into exciting, danger-filled ones, just like Wonder Woman's.

There's something magical in watching the transformation of a bespectacled, uniformed, plain Jane into an exotically beautiful, brightly costumed superwoman who is as deft in repelling bullets with her silver bracelets as her counterpart is with a steno pad. Lynda is convinced her portrayal is meaningful because she tries to show that "a woman doesn't have to be unattractive to be independent." And she does it in her own unique way.

"I have welded the two so much that there are things about myself and the values I have that the character has," Lynda says. "Diana Prince is probably more me than Wonder Woman is because, obviously, Wonder Woman is a fantasy and Diana is more a human being. And I wear glasses, too."

Though her acting has been called limited by some, and her skills rudimentary by others, Lynda does do most of her own stunts. She's a natural athlete, a former swimming champ, tennis player, ballet student, and constant dieter (when she first saw herself in her Wonder Woman costume, she immediately went on a diet and lost ten pounds. She felt a lot better for it, although nobody even noticed any difference).

Lynda trained long and hard with one of the top stuntmen in Hollywood to learn just how to land correctly; to throw her golden lasso so that it hits the mark; and how to use her arms and turn correctly so she could deflect enemy missiles. It was an arduous, sometimes even torturous program, but Lynda's physical skills and excellent condition made her a fast and able student. She's really the only one of the super duper women on TV who does so much of her own stunt work. Lindsay Wagner had a professional for the really difficult stunts her role demands; the Angels and Angie Dickinson rely much less on the real physical stuff than Lynda does—although they are all in top condition.

Lynda puts in a 12-15 hour day on the set—

there are a lot of costume and set changes—but her life is not all work and no play. She manages to keep up her tennis and swimming and spends as much time as possible with her husband. Either she has more energy than all the rest of the super-women on TV put together, or she's just not as vo-cal about her complaints: Lynda is one of the few series stars who doesn't usually mention how little time she has to live her life because of her work schedule. She frequently has only about a week to study each script, sometimes while filming at the same time.

Lynda and Ron had a true delayed love-at-first sight reaction to each other. Their first meeting wasn't a bell ringer, although they felt the good vibes even then. It was at an ABC party in 1975, and there were just so many people there, it was quite impossible to get to say more than "Hi, how are you?" to anyone. Ron was there with his star client, Lindsay Wagner; he had been—quite suc-cessfully—devoting all his time and effort to her career. There were rumors raging at the time about whether Lindsay would marry Ron or her long-time boyfriend, Michael Brandon, and the odds were about evenly divided. Ron and Lynda didn't really get to meet until a year later, when he turned up on the "Wonder Woman" set to visit a friend.

"I looked at Lynda and I just said 'Wow!'" Ron remembers.

"He asked if we could have lunch," Lynda says. "We did, and right at the beginning, I asked him if this was business or pleasure. He said that I was certainly someone who spoke her mind. It turned out that his business was pleasure. How could it be otherwise? Ron is so lovable, and he's such a genius when it comes to managing talent.

"Ron is a gorgeous man, and I've never been so in love with anyone before."

And Ron is equally enthusiastic about his woman. "It shakes me up. I'm very much in love with Lynda. I love her more than anything. I look after Lindsay Wagner's interests 24 hours a day. . . and I love Lynda Carter 24 hours a day."

Quite a busy schedule for Mr. Samuels, and one, some think, he's not juggling as well as he might. "He's so blinded by his love for Lynda," an acquaintance said, "that he hasn't got much interest for anything else. . . . He's just too busy to be where he's needed."

None of his clients are complaining, though, and Mr. and Mrs. Samuels just ignore the taunts. They are, it's true, totally wrapped up in one another, learning and growing and making their marriage a solid one. When they were first making wedding plans, Ron announced to the world, "I feel as if we're married already. I'm more married to Lynda than I could possibly be to any other human being as long as I live. We are emotionally married. I respect her. I'm committed to her. And I love her."

In much the same love-filled tone of voice, Lynda gushed, "I'd much rather spend time alone with Ron talking than anything else. There are so many things to learn about someone you're in love with. It's intriguing. It's an adventure. It's a mystery. I don't know if I can ever know Ron entirely. He is such a growing person, he is constantly changing.

"I was looking for someone strong and gentle without being macho," Lynda continues. "Someone I could rely on." All of Lynda's dreams were fulfilled when she met Ron. Lynda and Ron are totally together on just about everything, and have been from the very day they took their wedding vows.

It was a perfect California morning, blue skies, birds singing, glorious sunshine. Only family and a few close friends were there—neither Ron nor Lynda wanted their wedding day to be a free-for-all. The service was non-denominational, written mostly by Lynda and Ron themselves, although a minister did officiate. And for all of Lynda's modern thinking and independent spirit, when it came to the wedding, tradition had a very major place. She wore a beautiful Mexican wedding dress in off white and came down the aisle on the arm of her father. Standing up for her, as the maid of honor, was her sister, Pam. The best man was Ron's very good friend, George Litt, who also volunteered his gorgeous house and gardens for the ceremony and party that followed. The actual ceremony was brief, but beautiful, and those closest to the altar say that both Lynda and Ron had tears in their eyes as they said their "I do's."

After the ceremony, and after Lynda had tossed her bouquet into the crowd, there was a Mexican-style fiesta, complete with a strolling Mariachi band. Lynda and Ron spent a glorious weeklong honeymoon in Hawaii before the demands of both their careers brought them back to Hollywood.

Despite Lynda's work schedule, she tries to be domestic. She loves to cook and to be at home, and the Samuels' have tried to arrange their time so that most—if not all—of their evenings are free to be together. Children are in the future. They want a few, definitely, but not until they've had a few years to themselves first. Lynda says she'd quit show business before she'd let her career threaten her marriage. "I'd follow Ron to the ends of the earth," she says.

It's easy to see that Lynda loves married life. It may be a bit harder for them to find the same kind of time to spend together as they had when they first met—Lynda was on a break from filming then —but they work at it.

"We really take the time to talk with—not at— each other," Lynda says joyfully. "Because if we don't make the time, it's never going to be there.

"Ron is so cute! He's my first and only love. I wake up in the morning and he's there and I get a little something in my heart that I've never experienced before. It's sharing wins and frustrations and all of that. Sharing is the best part. It's not so much of what it is in particular, but helping one another out of their frustrations."

Lynda Carter was dating a lot of people when she met Ron, but none of them was for real. She wants this romance with Ron to go on forever. He gives her a great feeling of security. They are both strong-willed individuals, but Ron seems to see the total picture when Lynda is looking at just one little element. So it works out just fine; there may be an occasional "battle of the wills," but they complement each other's thinking perfectly.

"Lynda is a beautiful, beautiful person," her husband says glowingly. "Not just physically, but in every way. She is absolutely everything I ever wanted in a human being."

It's clear that the feeling is mutual. Lynda has that special glow in her eyes everytime she talks about Ron, and she keeps telling anyone who'll listen, "This is the most wonderful thing that's ever happened to me."

It's a perfect love story. Between her husband and her career, Lynda Carter seems to have found true happiness.

"Wonder Woman" is a smooth, professional production with a proven track record. Lynda is called on more to exhibit her physical prowess than her acting talents, and if she's not quite ready for an Oscar, at least she's brought some human qualities to a superhuman character. No one can deny she's a beautiful woman who uses her well proportioned physique to its best advantage and does a pretty good job of providing a real live superheroine to her adoring public.

If Lynda has her way, and Ron's continuing help, you'll soon see another side of her talent. She has started writing songs again, picking up where she left off when she took up acting, and she's really thrilled to get back to it. "Music is the sleeper part of my life," says Lynda. "Something I love and really enjoy doing. It's just that I never had the opportunity, nor have I really wanted to do it before now. Now, I can do it with much more flair and a much bigger send off than I could have if I had never quit touring and began acting."

Lynda writes what she likes to call "top forty country," a cross between country and soft rock. She's putting together a nightclub act using mostly her own material, and she'll start breaking it in with personal appearances and concert dates around the country. Ron's already gotten her a recording contract and a future booking in Las Vegas. And that's only the beginning. Lynda's goal is to do as many different things as she can—to expand as an actress, to sing in nightclubs and on records, maybe even to try her feet at dancing. Great Hera! From superwoman to superstar in only two short years.

"Lynda has a lot more dimension than you see on 'Wonder Woman,' " her husband and mentor says proudly. "She has an IQ of almost genius, and she is one of the best singers in the world. And I'm overly critical."

Chapter 3
Lindsay Wagner

Turning Jaime Sommers into the bionic beauty didn't cost quite as much as remaking Steve Austin into "The Six Million Dollar Man." But since no one really wanted to call the show "The Four Million Eight Hundred and Seventy-Nine Thousand Dollar Girl," they settled for the "Bionic Woman" and left it at that.

Jaime first popped up as Steve's ex-fiancee on a two-part episode of "The Six Million Dollar Man." Despite the fact that by the end of Part II, Jaime had "died" in a sky-diving accident, the calls and letters about the character were so overwhelmingly in favor of her miraculous recovery and a happier ending that Jaime was given, through "revolutionary cryogenic techniques," a bunch of new parts—two legs, an arm, and an ear.

Even her fingernails are bionic—she can open a can of tuna fish with a literal snap of her fingers. She can also tear telephone books in half, punch a respectable hole in a brick wall, and lift a car to shoulder level. If anyone on TV is a true superwoman it's Jaime Sommers. Unlike her quick-change artist counterpart, Wonder Woman, Jaime doesn't need any special costume or protective armor to call on for her extraordinary strength; and again, unlike the Queen of the Amazons, Jaime's boyfriend—as well as the government—knows all about her fantastic powers.

Because parts of her body are government issue, she's under obligation to offer her bionic skills to the OSI in their constant battle to thwart gangsters, mobsters, foreign agents, and a general melange of garden-variety bad guys. The OSI is sort of a CIA-type organization, run by Oscar Goldman (Richard Anderson), who oversees the activities of both of the superpeople.

When ABC decided to drop "The Bionic Woman" (as they did with "Wonder Woman"), the show was quickly gobbled up by NBC. After a shaky start in the ratings, against some formidable competition, the show has finally found its place and fully intends to stay there. Lindsay's been promised some scripts with real meat to them, but so far all she has been thrown is a bone and a bionic dog to catch it.

It probably doesn't really make much difference. Lindsay's personality and sense of humor seem to show right through even the shakiest scripts.

Lee wasn't the happiest person in the world when the new series was first announced—Lindsay had gotten a super money deal that substantially topped his own. The inter-show visiting that was part of the original idea was cut down to a minimum. Whether it was because, as rumored, Lee absolutely refused to have anything to do with "The Bionic Woman" or not has never been fully explained, but Jaime, along with her new parts, was given some memory damage and a few little brain cell injuries. So she only remembers Steve "with my head, not my heart." Now that "The Bionic Woman" is on NBC, there's no question of a continuing romance between the two. The only real link between the shows is the character of Oscar Goldman.

The series is, after all, a fantasy in the good old-fashioned comic strip tradition. They are both pretty simple, sort of like the old-time adventure serials that made Saturday afternoon at the movies every kid's dream world. Lindsay gets to do one of her superhuman feats of strength and endurance about every 15 minutes or so, and the effort is exhausting. "The series demands the sort of actual exertion and preparation I've never known before," she says. "A stunt girl does the really heavy, impossible acts—like long jumps and pushing over cars, but the camera has to catch me either initiating the actions or completing them. When the Bionic Woman jumps, I must be seen landing. I have to start pushing over the car or breaking open the door. Consequently, I've developed all sorts of muscles in my arms and legs that I never thought I had."

For Lindsay, "The Bionic Woman" was a big break. She spent a lot of years practicing her craft, almost from the moment she could walk. In a way, she almost had to: her childhood years were filled with insecurities and searchings for love—and for her father.

When Lindsay was born, in Los Angeles on June 22, 1949, to Bill and Marilyn Wagner, they were one happy family. The Wagners doted on each other and gave their baby daughter all the love and attention they possibly could. But they were young and hadn't really grown up yet, and they were just not ready or able to deal with the responsibility of a child, even one as pretty and lovable as Lindsay. She became the victim, although unwittingly, of their delayed maturity; when Marilyn and Bill were divorced, in 1958, Lindsay was only nine, but she felt "stranded." She adored her father, and he adored her as well, and she missed him terribly. She was desperately unhappy. "She blamed herself for the break-up of our marriage," Lindsay's mother says. "She told me, 'He doesn't love me or he wouldn't have gone away.' She took the responsibility."

That's not an uncommon thing for a young child whose parents split up to do. Lindsay was too young to understand that divorce usually has nothing to do with love for a child, there are many other factors involved. She was particularly sensitive and just couldn't muster up the emotional strength required to handle the situation. "She cried a lot as she grew up, but she never did know why she was crying," her mother goes on. "She only knew she wanted to cry. Lindsay would come home from school and cry. She would cry in the night and I would wake up and comfort her. I could never understand why a child so beautiful and with so much going for her should want to cry as much as she did."

Obviously, all the beauty, friends, brains, and even a comforting mother couldn't make up for all the loneliness Lindsay felt without her dad. Her mother even called her ex-husband and asked him to talk with Lindsay and try and make her understand. They sat together for hours, Lindsay crying while her father tried to make her feel better and help her see that it isn't always possible for two people to stay together forever, no matter how much it hurts.

In a newspaper interview, Bill Wagner, who is a professional photographer specializing in children's pictures, recalled one specific incident that happened about two years after the divorce. Marilyn had remarried by this time a man named Ted Ball, and she, her husband, and Lindsay pulled up in their car next to Bill at a traffic light. When Lindsay saw her father, she immediately stuck her head out the window and asked him to come and have dinner with them. "Marilyn and I looked at each other, and she began to cry. I drove off and the tears ran down my face," Bill Wagner remembered the afternoon not without a trace of those tears, 20 years later. "She really had tugged at my heartstrings, and I will never get over that moment."

The divorce, for all its traumas and heartbreaks, did have its brighter side: it got Lindsay interested in acting. Acting helped her to feel more secure: it allowed her to become someone else and never have to reveal her true feelings to anyone. She could forget her own problems and just get up on a stage and pretend.

Lindsay was, by age fourteen, tall (she was already 5′ 7″ by age 10, and is now 5′ 9″) and had the perfect shape and face to model college clothes for magazines and Diet-Rite soda for TV commercials. She hated it. She thought it was degrading, but she was reluctant to give it up. "So many people would have loved to be doing what I was doing, so I felt guilty about quitting," she says.

Lindsay had begun studying dancing with Joby Best, but she was "too inhibited" to keep it up and switched to acting lessons with Joby's husband, James. He trained her right, she says. "He taught me everything about my craft but refused to let me start acting when I was young. " 'Now you know the techniques,' he said, 'Go out and study people; find out what the characters you'll play are like. You don't learn much about people growing up as an actress.' "

She followed his advice, including not accepting a role in a TV series at that time, and years later, when she did start acting professionally, she was ready because of it.

When the Ball family moved to Portland, Oregon, Lindsay went with them. She started practicing her acting on an amateur level at David Douglas High School. By all accounts, she was a sensation, no matter what part she played, delivering her lines with such intensity and conviction hardly anyone dared believe she wasn't speaking

41

the absolute truth. As Jean, in "Stage Door," one of her most prophetic parts, Lindsay emoted, "I'm going to leave this town and when I come back, I'm going to be big, really big." She did exactly that, didn't she? She worked hard, did a little modeling when she could and even gave up an adoring boyfriend to follow her star.

Giving up one boyfriend was not a big problem for Lindsay because she had so many. Her beauty attracted men of all ages, but her real problem was convincing them she had a brain.

She attended the University of Oregon for a year, then six months at Mt. Hood Community College in Portland. But Lindsay had enough of being a student. She dropped out and joined a rock group—one so bad they lasted two nights in Dallas and broke up. That was enough of being a singer (she would come back to that later). In 1968 she went back to Hollywood and was a little "freaked out"—the emotional scars of her childhood had not yet healed enough for her to get everything together. It took three long years of soul-searching and putting her life in perspective before she was able to shape up enough to land a part that got her even a little attention. It was a small role, her first professional appearance, in an episode of "Marcus Welby, M.D." Monique James, then in charge of the New Talent Development department at Universal, saw the show and signed Lindsay to a $162.00 a week contract. That was in 1971. Over the next four years, Lindsay was always working, although in small parts, but on top shows: "Owen

Marshall," "Night Gallery," "The Bold Ones," and three more "Marcus Welby" episodes. She made three movies: "The Paper Chase," "Two People" with Peter Fonda, and a Canadian film, "Second Wind."

But by the time Lindsay got the part as Jaime Sommers in "The Six Million Dollar Man," Universal had let her contract lapse. Luckily, she had a smart manager, Ron Samuels. When it was decided to resurrect Jaime for another two episodes of "The Six Million Dollar Man," Samuels asked for $25,000 each. He never expected to get it, but he did, as well as a handsome deal for the new series that grew out of it: $5 million in five years; a five feature film a year guarantee, plus a nice 12½ percent royalty on any Bionic Woman by-product, dolls, posters, etc. His clever maneuvering made him a super agent with clients like Jackie Smith, Jennifer O'Neill, and Lindsay's husband, Michael Brandon, actor-screenwriter, producer who she married in December 1976.

It was the second time around for Lindsay. The first, to music publishing executive Allan Ryder, didn't last very long, and Lindsay never talks about it. The pain and frustration of the divorce made her wary of marrying again. "We have such a nice relationship now," Lindsay said in early 1976, "we wonder if marriage would mess it up. Now is the time to maintain a sense of yourself instead of becoming dependent. We keep talking about marriage, and don't do it. I have a feeling it's going to be one of those now or never situations when the time comes." Another prophetic Wagner statement. Just a few months later, they decided it was now.

They had first met in an acting class given by director Milton Katzelas, in March 1975. "I sat down next to Lindsay one day and we began talking," Michael remembers vividly. "When the class was over, I suggested we go out to dinner. She said she wasn't able to, but asked me to ring her the next day." But Michael had to go to Hawaii to do a film, and they didn't get to see each other again for several months until they met accidentally in Carmel. He asked her to come live with him at his ranch; she accepted. Their days were happy, playful ones, full of their togetherness and sharing: riding bareback over the ranch's forty acres, swimming, just being themselves. Their idyll ended when Lindsay got the series in January 1976. They hardly got to see each other anymore. Lindsay was working 12-16 hours every day. Michael had sold the ranch to Bob Dylan.

The long hours and constant activity were almost fatal. Michael says she must have been so dead tired from the week's work that she blacked out for a few seconds and nearly totaled her MG one morning. She came close to killing Michael and herself in the process. "Lindsay had a split lip and a slice in her skull. Her chest was bruised and cut where the steering wheel had gone into it," Michael recalls. "She was lucky—the steering wheel was completely bent and could have caused worse damage. She was only in the hospital for a few days. I was in surgery for five hours and in the hospital for weeks. The right side of my forehead was split open from the eye up. The eye itself was scratched. The nerves on that side of the forehead had been severed, and it took months until the feeling came back."

Lindsay remembers, not the physical pain, although it must have been considerable, but the shock of seeing Michael in the hospital and realizing "that I'd accidentally come close to killing off the person I loved most in the world."

The accident drew them closer into a mutually protective bond and thrust them closer towards marriage. When shooting for the first thirteen weeks of the series was finally over—there had been an understandable delay for a few weeks as Lindsay recuperated from the accident—Lindsay was so exhausted she knew she couldn't possibly do twenty-two more episodes unless she had some rest. So she and Michael went to Europe—they had thought about Aspen or Palm Springs but Lindsay really wanted to get away to someplace where no one would recognize her.

They landed in Cannes, and almost immediately Lindsay landed in the hospital, suffering from what the doctors called "second grade anemia, with complete physical and mental exhaustion." They kept her in the clinic a few days, building her strength up with vitamin shots. As soon as they could, she and Michael left the frenzy of the Riviera for the English countryside. It was the relaxation and rest Lindsay needed. She was able to return to work fortified not only by their days in Europe but by Michael's own strength and understanding.

By December 1976, Lindsay and Michael felt they had been together long enough to realize that their relationship was only getting better and better as the days went by. It was an extension of everything that had been going on between them since they had met. "Admittedly," Lindsay says, "there had been a pattern in my past life: I'd never been with a man more than two years without splitting up. Michael the same. Yet, here we were, at the end of two years, telling each other that we were more in love than ever.

"We felt we really knew each other, and we learned we could grow together. We believed each of us had the qualities the other was looking for in a mate. There was the knowledge that each had the ability to make decisions about the other under pressure—learning how we behaved in uncomfortable situations."

Those are pretty strong grounds to build a marriage on. The romantic elements were there from the beginning, and always will be. Michael is everything Lindsay needs and has been looking for in a man. He was a Gestalt therapist before he turned to acting, and he has a flexible, understanding nature, plus strength and compassion to match. He is good for Lindsay; he keeps her feet on the ground and helps prevent her popularity and fame from overwhelming her. She has a tendency to be a bit manic when things are going either too well or too badly, but he is definitely a calming, soothing influence.

Yet their wedding might never have taken place had Michael not agreed to go through a three-day training course at the Arica Institute in New York City. Lindsay had discovered the spiritual teachings of Arica four years ago, when her first marriage ended. "Arica is involved in the study of many different forms of energy working on the psyche," Lindsay explains, "increasing spirituality and maintaining mental balance. It's not a religion. It's very scientific and metaphysical." Arica is one of the many groups that claim to help its members increase their spiritual awareness, and Lindsay wears the Arica symbol around her neck—a pentagonal shape that indicates the different patterns of energy. Wherever they have lived, Lindsay has always had an almost empty separate room where she meditates each morning for twenty minutes before leaving for work. The meditation, she says, "opens my mind to the flow of the quality of the day." It's another part of the Arica program.

While Lindsay herself has always had a strong sense of God, Michael needed Arica to get him to "trust in God's energy and my own. It works."

"We have a sense of God in ourselves and in each other," says Lindsay. "I could never marry a man I couldn't relate to in a spiritual sense, neither could I marry anyone who wasn't interested in growing and bending the way I feel I am." Obviously, the man she did marry was the perfect choice. The wedding took place in the Founder's

Church of Religious Science in Los Angeles. It was small and quiet, only family and a few friends, with Lindsay's half-sister, Randall, who's 14, as the maid of honor, and Michael's grandfather, who is 90, as his best man.

Michael wanted to drive to the church in a "vintage" touring car, but Lindsay said no. She also made sure that there was no press coverage and no throngs of fans around the church. Her wedding was "too important to be turned into a circus."

Both her parents were there, and for her father, seeing Lindsay's happiness was like a salve to his own painful memories of the traumas of her childhood the divorce caused. His tears, this time, were tears of joy that his daughter had at last found peace of mind.

The service included a special ceremony built around three candles: one for Lindsay, one for Michael, and the third a symbol of their oneness. Together, they lit the last candle with the other two and then extinguished their individual flames. It was a beautiful ritual that emphasized their life to be as one entity.

The ceremony and their years together have made what they share a very special thing. "I'm his woman," Lindsay says proudly.

"To me it was bestowing of an honor never before given. I never met anybody worth doing it with before. I felt she was just that person," says Michael.

"It's Lindsay who really puts their relationship in perspective. "We've grown to know each other truly well, to avoid creating blocks or inhibiting the other person's growth as an individual. We worked at eliminating barriers that might exist between us."

Michael is no slouch. He's constantly working on a script of some kind for movies or TV. He has recently sold a play. He even submitted a script for "The Bionic Woman," a two-parter with himself as Jaime Sommers' love interest. He starred in "Red Alert," with William Devane, and on several TV specials like "Red Badge of Courage," and "James Dean: Portrait of a Friend." He is determined never to be known as "Mr. Wagner."

"Michael has handled the sudden publicity, fame, and attention that came into my life with 'The Bionic Woman.' He was mature enough not to let it interfere with our relationship. So many things have happened so fast, but there wasn't a negative response from him, which I had secretly feared."

If anything, the show—besides the money and fame—has brought Lindsay and Michael closer together, even if it is for shorter periods of time, and not always in private. "There are moments when fame gets in the way," Lindsay moans. "It's annoying when we can't spend a nice quiet evening mooning at each other over dinner without having somebody ask for an autograph. But it's part of the price you pay."

So the happy couple tries to spend as much time alone as possible in their secluded estate in Coldwater Canyon. It's lushly furnished with the antique reproductions Michael prefers because they're less expensive than the originals. Those originals they do have he claims Lindsay overpays for because dealers raise their prices when they see her coming. There's the mandatory pool, of course, always kept at near-body temperature for their midnight swimming. They have a dog, Pooka, a golden retriever. Lindsay also owns some property on the Washington-Oregon border, near the Hood River, that they'd like to work on. There's almost 160 acres and an old house with no electricity or running water, and no time to fix it up. They'd also like to buy some land in Idaho, near where they spent their honeymoon, but again, time seems to get in the way.

Lindsay's day begins at 7:00, she meditates before she leaves and manages to get in some breakfast, sometimes, between make-up and hair-do on the set. She's usually home by 7:00 to cook dinner. "I'm a darn good cook," she claims. "I'm dynamite with old-fashioned meals like pot roast with potatoes, carrots, and onions; I'm good with gravies and sauces, and I'm really great with turkey dinners."

She manages, despite that, to stay skinny (she weighs about 124 pounds), mostly because of those long active hours on the set (last year, they were even longer, nearly 16 hours a day, but this season she insisted that they be more reasonable). She's not into competitive sports at all (nor is Michael) and never has been. At school, she used any excuse to get out of gym. She blames this partially on her father, who was a semi-pro football player and took her to football games every weekend (he had counted on having a son to name Lindsay) and partially on the fact that she never had a typical young girl's childhood. "I was always with older people," she says. "I was always minding other children: my sister, Randy, and my aunt's child. I never was very physical. I was a stuffy kid; I didn't even listen to rock and roll until I was twenty. Now I'm having a ball running around and doing the various physical things I have to do for the series."

One thing the series is making Lindsay do is postpone having children. She loves kids and loves working with them on the show. She has added a lot of her own ideas to her role as Jaime Sommers, teacher, like conducting the class in a circle so everyone could participate and no one could hide out in the back of the room.

Before she married Michael, Lindsay thought she might like to be a single parent. But her thinking has changed. She has an awful lot to give, and she wants to be able to give it totally. She's a believer in what she calls "pre-natal influences," and she'd never want her children to suffer from the divided attentions combining motherhood and a career might result in. She's sure her first child will be a boy: she dreamt it would be when she was a child. Michael wants to have a beautiful little girl, "who looks just like Lindsay." Whichever, it won't be for at least another year or two.

So now she's devoting her time and energy to her husband and career and hoping that soon she and Michael can do a film together. She'll produce; he'll direct; and they'll both star. They've already done one project together, a TV special called "Lindsay Wagner: The Other Side of Me." It aired on ABC, and it was something Ron Samuels (who also produced it) had arranged while Lindsay was still with ABC. It was not a critical success. Lindsay sang a little, danced a little, pretended she was Esther Williams and Queen Guenevere. Her singing and dancing both left a lot to be desired; and Michael, as King Arthur, was not exactly shining. But they did look like they were having a good time together, and presumably, that's what really counts.

If there's been any big change in either of the Brandons since their marriage, they feel that it's other people seeing them differently. They haven't changed, although Lindsay says she does see Michael in a slightly different light. "I find him to be a very rare man. He has the qualities of an older man (he's 32). I used to date older men primarily because I like the maturity, patience, and understanding they had to offer. The willingness to say, 'Hang on, it isn't the end of the world.' Older men take care of things the moment they come up. Michael understands that."

It might be that Lindsay was really searching for a father substitute in those older men, and perhaps that is very true. But Michael, although he takes care of his woman, is no pseudo-father. He's very much the modern man, deeply in love with his wife. And Lindsay knows just where she's at, too. Her acting is her therapy, and it makes her feel as if she's getting younger.

"I was old when I was a kid, and I grew backwards," she says. Now she has a rare combination of the freedom of youth and the maturity to be responsible for her own actions. And she has got a man who not only loves her but gives her the kind of support and energy she needs to make the two work together.

"I always believed there wasn't anything I couldn't get if I wanted it enough and worked hard enough," she says with a bionic glint in her eye.

Chapter 4
Kate Jackson

It's the supershow with superbudget and three of the most superwomen to ever hit the TV screen!

Whoever thought, in 1976, that this unpretentious little detective series called, of all things, "Charlie's Angels," would capture the kind of audiences that only the World Series and the Super Bowl ever did?

It all started with an idea from Spelling-Goldberg, who had already given the world "The Rookies," "Starsky & Hutch," and "S.W.A.T." They'd add a little "stunning beauty" to the gruff, male-oriented action-adventure shows and see what happened.

What happened was the biggest, most expensive, most successful smash series in TV history. It hit the Nielsen Top 10 its first week. It's still there, a new season and another new Angel later.

Collectively, "Charlie's Angels," past and present, probably have the most hair, the most teeth and the highest salaries of any other women in television; and more time and money is spent on hairdressers and wardrobe than any other part of the production.

The producers wanted a show about "three karate-chopping types" who worked for a private detective. They got it, but not immediately. Their first proposal was rejected, and the project was shelved for a year. Then ABC got their new president of entertainment, Fred Silverman. Not only did he like the idea for the show, he liked the idea of putting more women on TV in active parts. Get three gorgeous females, give them gorgeous clothes and just enough brute strength to make them believable as private eyes, and do it.

The world was ready for a little glamour and glitter, and Farrah Fawcett, Kate Jackson, and Jaclyn Smith gave them plenty. So much, in fact, that more than half the TV sets in the United States were tuned to ABC every Wednesday night at 10:00. Twenty-three million men, women, and children: truck drivers, corporate executives, interior designers, ditch diggers, you name it, were watching. They still do. Farrah's gone, but so what? Nobody seems to miss her, and Cheryl Ladd has almost as many teeth and a full head of her own beautiful hair.

There's only one man on the show. Charlie's nothing but a disembodied voice—belonging to actor John Forsyth—who makes terrible, double-entendre jokes over the phone. The real man of the hour is Bosley, played by the slightly rotund, naturally good-humored, David Doyle. He offsets Charlie's crude attempts at raunchy humor with a quiet dignity that gives the show the little bit of class it has.

So what's it like being the only man surrounded by three fabulous superfemales? Doyle jokes about it a lot, but he is, as he puts it, "one happy man." "We have three intelligent, good-looking women for starters, and their cohort—me—is intelligent and conventionally attractive. A man and three women. We're all on equal footing as regards authority, ability, and intelligence. It makes for a very good tennis match, and it's a lot of fun."

One mortal man. Three super women. It's an unbeatable combination.

*   *   *   *

Of all the Angels, it has been said that only Kate Jackson can really act. She *is* the only actress on the series with any *real* experience and training. And, the series *was* her vehicle after "The Rookies" was cancelled.

When Spelling-Goldberg's "The Rookies" was cancelled Kate was available. The producers held her option, but they didn't seem to be doing a whole lot about it. She called them and asked for a meeting to discuss her future. They tossed around a lot of ideas, and Leonard Goldberg suggested a series about three Avengers-type women—Emma Peels in bikinis and bluejeans who worked for a man named Harry. It was Kate who made the vital contribution to the brainstorming session. She saw a picture on Aaron Spelling's wall of three angels and noticed the complicated and elaborate telephone system on his desk. . . . "Suppose they work for a detective," she said, "and he talks to them via a squawk box. . . ." She got up and paced around the room—you know how it is when you're trying to think of something—"How about 'Harry's Angels?' " And so a show was born. Harry gave way to Charlie because there already was "Harry O," David Janssen's show, on the air.

The role of Sabrina Duncan—the most intellectual and brainy of the Angels, and their unofficial leader, was a much different one from Kate's role as Nurse Jill Danko on "The Rookies." As Sabrina, Kate gets to act more, work more, and learn more. Sabrina is a sophisticated woman, brought up in Europe and multi-lingual, but of course, any evidence of that background is because Kate plays her that way and not because it's particularly written into the script.

The confidence to build a character is something Kate learned from watching and observing other professionals at work. From her first major role, in ABC's supernatural soap opera, "Dark Shadows," in which for the first two months she played Daphne Harridge, a "silent ghost," and didn't have one word of dialogue to her first speech, "about a mile long" as she remembers it, she was always observing. During that first speaking scene, a little kid in the cast started jumping up and down on her long gown. She just went on saying her lines, never realizing her gown was on fire and the little trouper was busily stamping it out.

During her four years on "The Rookies," it was pretty much the same kind of thing. She didn't have many big parts, except when she was being kidnapped—which seemed to happen fairly often as Kate recalls—so it was another case of stand by and learn (as a matter of fact, when ABC scheduled "The Rookies" for late night re-runs, if anything ever needed to be cut for time, it was usually Kate). She was really just the token female on the series: the perfect subservient wife who boosted her husband's ego with constant adoration. Her parts were usually just emotional fill between the police chases and bullets.

With Sabrina came Kate's first chance to really prove herself as an actress, and she went at it with the tough, analytical energy that has since become her trademark. "I bought a stack of books on crime," says Kate. "I wasn't so much interested in technique as I was in trying to find out why an attractive young woman like Sabrina would want to be a policewoman. All three of the girls in the series quit the police academy in order to be private detectives. Why would they do that?"

Excitement? Glamour? Danger? The challenge of excelling in a traditionally masculine role while still retaining their femininity? Probably all those things. And in Sabrina's case, it was a little bit of a chance to prove she was more than just a pretty face and a beautiful body. "From my own readings and my own experiences, I fashioned a character that goes beyond the superficial draft that comes out of the network press kit," Kate says. "Sabrina is more likely to laugh than to cry; she's tough and she spends a good deal of time thinking about consequences. I have to try and get things like that into a script."

Kate tackles everything she does with that same kind of determination. Take for example, her choice of career. It wasn't an idle decision. "It's not that I wanted to be an actress, I had to be an actress," says the invincible Kate. "It wasn't the money or the fame. It's just that I want to be somebody. If I had stayed in my home town, I could have lived and died there and maybe nobody would have noticed me. I guess what I wanted to prove is that I am alive. It's a statement that I exist. I guess I want to make waves, make some noise, and call attention to myself."

As a kid in Birmingham, Alabama, her parents' garage was her land of make-believe where she put on shows for the whole neighborhood. By the time she was eleven, the dream of bright lights and stardom had taken a firm hold—even if she now says that she would never have acknowledged it at the time. She started to really get seriously involved in high school, Birmingham's best, the all-girls Brooke Hill School, acting in plays and fantasizing about someday seeing her picture on the cover of a fan magazine—a dream that has certainly come true, in spades. According to some, Kate was quite the cut-up, indulging in all sorts of teen-age pranks—some funny, some malicious. Her high school drama teacher doesn't remember Kate as being particularly outstanding in that class, but friends recall her doing some hysterically funny, although rather cruel, imitations of her teachers. She was, apparently, more devil than angel; but nonetheless a serious student with good grades. Sounds like Kate was a pretty typical kid in high school, fun to be around, always thinking up new ways to put a little excitement into her life. College was next, but it wasn't purely the quest for knowledge that spurred her on. She followed her high school beau to the University of Mississippi. She was a good student, but college life was not the same kind of fun and games high school was. It was serious stuff. And she began to discover that her boyfriend and her studies were not as satisfying as she thought they would be. She wanted more. Her decision to leave school and her man was one of the gutsiest things she's ever done. "That last afternoon, as I was sitting at 'Ole Miss' with my studyboard on my lap, I thought, uh, uh, this is not getting it," Kate remembers. "I'm going to graduate with a major in history and good grades—so what?"

What she really wanted to do was to go to New York and study acting. She didn't get there directly but stopped off in Vermont to do a season of summer stock. And then it was on to New York where she immediately enrolled in the distinguished American Academy of Dramatic Arts.

It wasn't the easiest of transitions for the soft-voiced young Southern girl whose deceptive drawl and good manners masked a fierce independence and a complex, driving determination to succeed. It wasn't another school vacation, New York, it was real life. And it was rough. Kate worked hard, appearing in such Academy productions as "Night Must Fall," "The Constant Wife," and "Little Moon of Alban." At the same time, she was trying to support herself with an odd assortment of jobs. Kate's family wasn't sending her a life-giving check every month, so she worked for her rent money. "I couldn't type or take shorthand, so I modeled bridal gowns on Seventh Avenue. There, I learned a lot about Matzoh Balls. I never knew the meaning of real disdain until a counterman in a Jewish delicatessen withered me with a look when I asked if he could please cut the crusts off my pastrami on white with mayonnaise and lettuce." Kate laughs as she remembers what came next. . . . "I was also a 'turrific' tour guide at NBC for a while. I gave a great show in the old Inner Sanctum studios, complete with creaking door, rain, thunder, the works. Little old ladies pressed quarters into my palms, though they weren't supposed to tip. I worked in a ski resort for a while, too, straightening bent nails."

What she did mostly, though, was study—not just acting but her favorite actress—idol, if you will —Katharine Hepburn. Kate used to stand in front of Hepburn's house, pretending to wait for the bus. She knew every move her idol made to and from her home from Broadway, where she was starring in "Coco." "I'd knock on her door, leave flowers and run away," Kate says. "One day I got caught by her secretary, Phyllis, who asked my name, but I ran. I got caught again, and Phyllis said, 'Miss Hepburn insists on knowing who you are.' Well, if

Hepburn insists—right? I got a long letter from her, thanking me, on real stationery with her whole name embossed—Katharine Houghton Hepburn. Wow! I was too embarrassed to ever go back."

It's a rather charming story and indicative of Kate, shy and fragile but plucky and determined at the same time. Her infatuation with Hepburn and her respect and admiration for her talents is still strong. When Hepburn came to L.A. to star in "A Matter of Gravity," Kate was in the first row on opening night, along with a theatre full of other adoring fans. This was for Kate the realization that she wasn't the only person who loved Hepburn— but she swears that the star looked right at her in the opening scene. It was during the same week Hepburn opened that the Angels made their first national magazine cover. Kate wanted to send her idol a copy, but chickened out at the last minute. Instead, she just revels in the fact that they both have the same first name (although Kate was named Kate, not Katharine, after her grandmother), are both Scorpios, born a week and many years apart, and that both their home addresses have the same set of numbers in them. Little enough to build a dream on, but as Kate says, "I'd be eternally grateful if one of my dreams came true and I could share the smallest part of her kind of greatness."

Kate Jackson could be on her way. Her studies at the Academy paid off. She got a year-long stint on "Dark Shadows" and began developing herself careerwise, intellectually, and emotionally. She was building confidence along with ability. When Rene

Valente, then a talent scout, now the vice-president of Columbia Pictures Television, suggested she try Hollywood, Kate packed up and headed West. She made a lot of guest appearances—"The Jimmy Stewart Show," "Bonanza," and ABC made-for-TV movie called "The New Healers," and probably most importantly, at least in one respect, a Movie of the Week, "The Killer Bees," starring Gloria Swanson and Kate's boyfriend-to-be, Edward Albert.

It was 1971. Kate was doing "The Rookies," but her contract was generous and allowed her time out for other things. She had made a big splash in the gossip columns, dating Robert Evans, then Paramount chief, who had just divorced Ali MacGraw. It was really nothing serious. She went to the Academy Award presentations with him and laughed at the cruel jibes of reporters who intimated that Evans was merely using her as a substitute for his lost wife. Kate was flattered rather than upset by all the commotion. She was secure, and she knew she had been honest about her end of the relationship, especially to herself. She brought that same uncompromising honesty to her two years with Edward Albert, which, in part, was probably what helped end it.

They met, romantically enough, on a plane—albeit a studio job specifically used to transport the cast of "The Killer Bees" from Los Angeles to San Francisco, where it was being filmed. She had planned to catch up on her reading during the flight, getting through some of the literary and current events magazines she subscribes to. When Edward sat down next to her any thoughts of such intellectual pursuits vanished. Edward was impressed with that very stack of reading matter, amazed that underneath that pretty exterior seemed to be some depth and substance. They talked for the entire trip and found out they had much in common. It only took a couple of dates for them to decide to be together, which they were for two years.

It looked to everyone like the perfect match. She was honest, sensitive, and intelligent, with a blossoming career. He was talented (he impressed everyone with his role as the blind young man in "Butterflies Are Free" and is an accomplished photographer), handsome, and an Oxford scholar. They both had an unpretentious zest for living and shared passions for riding, tennis, photography, books, talking, and laughing a lot.

Their idea of a perfect evening was sitting around at home and cooking dinner, or maybe going down to the Santa Monica pier to pitch horseshoes. When he starred in the Mark Taper production of "Hamlet," Kate was at rehearsals with him every night—not because she felt she had to, but because she wanted to. It was exciting and wonderful, and a learning and growing experience for both of them.

But it ended, that perfect match, and it took Kate quite a long while to get over it. She still, to this day, avoids discussing it too much: it's obviously still a painful subject, and she refuses to delve into the reasons for the breakup. "It stopped. That's really the crux of it," is about all she'll say on the matter. "Not only is it over, it's over because it didn't work. It's very funny with relationships that are finished. You really don't remember them at all.

"It was hard for me to work on a series—I was doing 'The Rookies' at the time Edward and I were together—and still have the proper amount of time to give to Edward."

Some friends felt it wasn't just a time problem, it was the difference in their approaches to their respective careers that finally broke them up. Kate was then, and still is, dedicated and ambitious—or "complex and driven," as one old friend put it. Her career is foremost in her mind. Edward, on the other hand, was career-oriented but not nearly as time-consumingly as Kate. A good role in a film or TV show occasionally, or a theatre run, satisfied him completely; he wasn't looking for a series or a long-time commitment.

Since she broke up with Edward, Kate has been more or less playing the field. She has been seen on the arm of such Hollywood bachelors as Warren Beatty—briefly, however, since Kate is smart enough, and self-protective enough, to have realized from the start that Warren the lady-killer could never offer her the kind of relationship she ultimately wants and needs. She's been around, too, with young actors like Gary Quist, Richard Hatch, and most recently, Dirk Benedict, who starred in "Chopper One," an ABC series that never got off the ground. Ironically, one of Dirk's most successful roles was as the blind boy in a production of "Butterflies are Free," the very same role that got Edward Albert's career off to such a beautiful start. They are all strong men, assured, ambitious, and directed ... qualities Kate not only admires but specifically searches out in her men.

Unfortunately, or perhaps, at this time in her life, fortunately, Kate doesn't really have the time to give or worry about her love life. She says, only half-jokingly, "My love life ain't what it used to be. I've stopped smoking and drinking and staying out late. I've got to discipline myself or the work would kill me." With a laugh, she adds, "My current sins are confined to soda pop. Poor me! But I'm sure having fun."

Kate's day begins at 5:30 AM, when she's picked up by the studio limousine and taken off to wherever the day's shooting is. And if she's still half-asleep through the ride, who could blame her?

It's a grind. The Angels work at least 12 hours a day, and it takes about seven grueling days to film each episode of "Charlie's Angels." The hectic schedule has left its mark on all of them. Two producers have fallen away from sheer exhaustion, and one of the directors suffered a heart attack. Kate often gets severe headaches from the combination of long hours and not enough sleep. Even the stoic Farrah had been known to break into tears from the strain.

After a full day's shooting, Kate is usually home somewhere between eight and ten. She likes to just sit and unwind for a little while, eat dinner, study the next day's script, and then to bed. She gets up at 4:30 each morning so she can have a little breakfast before she leaves for the studio. Weekends are a little better. Kate sleeps late, does her marketing, maybe gets in some tennis (she works with a coach and has never really given up her dream of some-day being a tennis pro), jogs with her dog, a Siberian husky named Catcher. She once told an interviewer that because of the Angels' schedule all she really has time for is "tennis and her shrink." She regrets ever having said that, or more precisely, she regrets that the interviewer didn't hear it as sarcastically as Kate meant it, or thought it would make better copy to treat it as a serious statement. Kate does find time to play. She dates but prefers her evenings "out" at home, playing the guitar or shooting pool. She'd much rather have dinner with friends than go to a big party. On hiatus from "Angels," Kate does a variety of vacation-type things. She might pack up her dog, her camping gear, and cameras and take off for the mountains or the desert for some therapeutic time away and alone. Or she might, as she did this past year, go to Aspen for some cross-country skiing. She's an ex-cellent downhill skiier, but cross-country is particu-larly appealing because she can take Catcher with her. It takes a lot of stamina, something Kate has proven she has plenty of. Even on vacation Kate is up and about early, nourishingly breakfasted by eight, ready to face the day with her usual en-thusiasm and energy. She'd like to buy a house in Aspen someday, as sort of a home base she could always retreat to, to get away from the presures of work.

Home for Kate these days is a comfortable, but hardly extravagant, apartment in Westwood. She has a beautiful house in Beverly Hills, but it was burglarized a couple of years ago, and Kate lost everything, including some things that were personally very valuable to her. She was heartbroken over it and decided then and there that she didn't want to take another chance—at least not for awhile—of building up another collection of valuables, whether personally or financially important. But the apartment isn't stark by any means—it's mostly crammed with books, as is her dressing room trailer on the set. All three Angels were offered color TV sets; Kate opted for bookshelves instead. And it is filled with posters of Impressionist paintings rather than the real thing. "I figured people would either think I like nice things, or that I didn't have the time, or that I'm really tacky," says Kate about the posters, and one gets the impression that she really doesn't care what people think. She likes them.

It's not that she can't afford the real thing. She gets paid more than the other Angels (which was supposedly a large bone of contention for Farrah, one of whose demands was an exorbitant sum of money per show, and which turned out to be merely a smoke screen for her real reasons for leaving), and she still gets some residuals from reruns of "The Rookies." It is true, though, that Jaclyn Smith, Farrah, and now Cheryl Ladd, earn more in residuals from their commercials than Kate could ever hope to see in salary alone. But she has chosen not to go the model route.

"The thought of being a star on a television series hasn't hit me yet," Kate says. "All I know is that I go to work every day and I'm sort of tired. I'm not extremely extravagant, so I don't buy things to impress people with what I've got. I see other people lose perspective a lot, so I guess that must mean I don't lose it easily. I think owning houses and cars and diamond rings is nice—but I'd rather go skiing."

That's pretty much Kate in a nutshell. And while it may not be one of Kate's specific goals in life, not to let Hollywood get to her either consciously or not, she has remained true to her basic beliefs. When she gets to feeling that her environment is running her life—it shows up in two basic symptoms, depression and weight loss, something that her 5'8", 124 pound frame really can't afford —she just takes herself off somewhere private, perhaps to her beloved desert if time allows, and thinks it all out. "Finding her center," she calls it. There was a time when Kate felt she was trying to be what other people expected her to be, and it wasn't a happy time. So she sat herself down and started to learn who Kate Jackson really was and just what she really wanted out of life. She emerged from this particular soul-searching few days able to enjoy herself as she was without being bored by her own company. She knows who she is rather than who she is supposed to be, and that makes dealing with life and other people a whole lot easier. It also makes looking at the future that much more pleasant.

"I've got the next three years carefully planned," Kate the dreamer says. "My future includes marriage and children. I'll stay with 'Charlie's Angels' a year or so more, but then I have these secret plans. When I'm 31, I want to get married. Absolutely. I still believe in marriage, but I want to time everything right. I don't want to mess anything up, make some poor man unhappy. I want my kids brought up properly. I want to be a good mother and still have my career. So I have to keep everything cool, tidy, and in proper timing. Once I have a family, I'll slack off a little."

Kate's plans don't quite include the specific man she plans to marry and have as the father to her children. He has yet to come into the picture, but Kate knows he's out there somewhere. She's not actively looking, more like waiting to be found. It removes the burden of guilt from her shoulders, and she's free to accept or reject any man without feeling guilty, which she does worry about. She points out a passage from one of her favorite authors, Lillian Hellman, and interprets it in her own way. Hellman wrote: "I am suspicious of guilt in myself and in other people. It's usually a way of not thinking or of announcing one's own fine sensibilities. The better to get rid of them fast. But about . . . the guilt that came from my own good luck, I'm still pleased because it led somewhere." Jackson's analysis: "Guilt is nowhere. Don't torture yourself with what was and what has happened; just observe and learn." That certainly applies to her attitude toward men. She went through a whole series of "Mr. Wrongs," and she can now patiently afford to wait for "Mr. Right" to come along. The whole Hollywood lifestyle is really not the best environment for a serious romance. Kate quotes friend Dustin Hoffman as saying, "If you live in Beverly Hills too long, you turn into a Mercedes." And she agrees that it's difficult to get a good perspective on life out there because everything you do own becomes a kind of status symbol, and the pressures of the TV and movie business make people nervous and scared.

"I'd like a one-to-one relationship," Kate will admit. "But I know how hard it is for one to work. I think on a scale of ten, the chances of actors and actresses making a personal relationship work are barely one." It doesn't stop a person from trying, but, as Kate goes on to explain, you can't always help the jealousy that often gets in the way of things. "You can love someone very much," she says wisely, "but the changes in your personality and emotional state can bust a relationship up very quickly. You see, actors are really sensitive, emotional people, with strong egos, and those egos make it hard for their relationships to work."

It sometimes makes it even harder for a relationship between an actor and a non-professional to work. There are few husbands or wives willing, or emotionally able, to take a total back seat to their spouse's front-page lives. And living in someone else's shadow is not how Kate wants her husband to live his life. So now, mostly, Kate is sitting back and taking it easy in the romance department. She's concentrating on her career.

She likes working on the Angels show and felt it was going to work right from the beginning—maybe not to the extent that they'd all become superstars, but definitely a success. She is quick to defend it against the sexism charges: "Not any more than Rock Hudson as McMillan. He's a handsome man. And Telly's supposed to 'lad-de-dah, baby.' Isn't that sexist?" And the characters themselves, at least from Kate's point of view, are much more than 8 x 10 glossies that move and talk. She thinks of her role as Sabrina as a stretching role, one that she can learn from, and she tries to make something warm, alive, and individual out of the character, even though she sometimes has to work with scripts that are less than inspiring. She gets along just fine with her co-Angels and was upset, but sympathetic, when Farrah left. She really didn't expect Farrah to carry out her threat, and she's concerned about whether the ex-Angel did the right thing. The three of them, Kate, Jaclyn, and Farrah, spent much of their free time on the set together, laughing and girl-talking—it was like being back in college again, with girlfriends to share experiences with. Kate pooh-poohs the notion that they didn't get along, although many stories have appeared in print suggesting that Kate wasn't all that unhappy when Farrah left. She just wants to stop talking about it, dragging up old stuff, and get on with the present. "Everybody knows when you look back you turn to salt," she says.

"The next thing I would like to do is a situation comedy," says Kate. She'd be good at it! "My favorite show is 'Laverne and Shirley,' but, unfortunately, I wasn't right for either of those two parts."

There is a very funny side to Kate. She has a sophisticated sense of humor, but there is a part of her that does funny things but doesn't always know they're funny. Grant Tinker, Mary Tyler Moore's husband, and producer of her show and other TV sit-coms, has encouraged Kate to try for comedic roles. She fully intends to. She did appear on a live Bob Hope special, "doing jokes," and the audience loved it. So did Kate.

What else does this talented young woman have in store for herself? (She once said that when she dreams, she surrounds herself with an aura, and then her dreams come true.) The Broadway stage, definitely. "I was scared of the theatre when I first started. I found I was more comfortable in front of a camera. But now maybe I'm ready to face the challenge of the stage. I get scared, but I get a tremendous rush. . . . I get so high and happy being scared. Giving everything you've got and making it work is the greatest kick. I once had the same rush of fright from the camera."

Movies? Whoops! They're another part of Kate's secret plans for the future, the ones she doesn't want to talk about too much. But she firmly believes something good is going to happen, or else she never would have mentioned it. She wants to produce her own TV film from a script she wrote about a young girl who runs away from home.

If you think Kate's ambitions are all centered in front of the audience, you'd be sorely mistaken. She'd very much like to do some writing (hopefully, the money she makes from the series will allow her to take some time off and do just that). "My mother is a writer—short stories and things," Kate says in a rare moment of discussing her family (mom's name is Ruth; dad's is Hogan, he is a building materials wholesaler. Her sister Jenny, younger by a couple of years, teaches school in Birmingham.) "She (her mother) is my greatest influence in that direction. Perhaps in a year I'll be ready to submit a script." If she gets the chance to offer scripts to the producers, it would certainly be an incentive to stay with "Angels" for a few more years; she'd sort of like to try her hand at directing, too, especially if the script is her own and she feels it just has to be done in a particular way. She has been around cameras and sets long enough to have a basic working knowledge, but she's not sure she has the instincts or the skills quite yet. But give her just a few more years. . . .

Kate has definitely seen some physical as well as emotional changes in herself since she's become an Angel. The most obvious, of course, is her hair. She is the only one on the series who doesn't have long, flowing tresses, although she did in the beginning. Kate simply felt that a short-haired Sabrina would convey the image she wanted to project— that of a liberated woman who's too involved with life and work to be a slave either to her hair or her looks. "I can touch my hair on this show," she says by way of explanation. "On 'The Rookies' people thought I had a stiff neck because I had to hold my head straight so that my hair wouldn't fall in my face. When I would forget, my hair would fall forward and I'd have to do the scene again because you couldn't see my face."

No more problems like that. Her sleek brown hair just naturally falls back into her blunt cut with just a toss of her head. But besides the new hairdo, Kate says her body has undergone some real changes—two years of physical aging for every year she's been in front of the cameras. She can see it when she watches some of "The Rookies" re-runs, and when she looks at old photos. Sometimes she can't believe it's the same Kate looking back at her. "I used to think when someone changed that much in a few years they had to have had something fixed. I haven't had anything done!"

Not that she's displeased with the alterations that nature has made. Quite the contrary. She likes the new "Kate Jackson" very much, both the physical changes and the psychological ones that have grown up alongside them. "I was a little girl when I started 'The Rookies,' " Kate says. "In just a few years there have been changes in my thinking, how I deal with things, and my level of sophistication."

It's hard to believe that Kate today, outspoken, assured, and brimming with confidence, used to be so shy and so self-conscious that she would go to industry functions and sit silently by herself. At one of those parties friend Suzanne Pleshette told Kate that she really ought to be saying something —her attitude of silence was just plain selfish. Kate agreed that maybe it was, but she has never been much for small talk. Our Kate finds it boring.

She's much more in touch with her feelings these days, and would just as easily tell someone she finds a conversation boring than sit back and grimly bear it, as she once did. It's a part of the growing up process that has brought Kate to the point in her life where she can seriously deal with her emotions, her wants, her needs—in other words, her life. The brainiest Angel (also, incidentally, the tallest and the highest paid) is the one with both feet planted firmly on the ground.

"I can't live like Holly Golightly the rest of my life," she says. (Holly was Truman Capote's flighty, fantastical heroine in "Breakfast At Tiffany's".) "It's like I've got a little angel on my shoulder. Strange I should end up an angel myself."

Charlie's new Angels and their cohort, Bosley: Cheryl Ladd, Jaclyn Smith, David Doyle, and Kate Jackson. They get along like four peas in a pod. *UPI*

When Prince Charles visited the States in October 1977, he made a special request to come to the studio and meet all the Angels. *UPI*

When Kate first started playing Sabrina, her hair was almost as long as Jackie and Farrah's. Her new short do is much freer. *Wide World*

Rumor has it that an Angels director was fired because he wouldn't give Catcher a speaking part. Kate says it's definitely not true. *Phil Roach, Photoreporters*

Kate co-starred with ex-Kung Fu hero David Carradine in a made-for-TV movie called "Thunder and Lightening" in the early seventies. *Frank Edwards, Fotos International*

Jackie says she doesn't look good in a bikini, but she sure wowed everyone in her racing suit at Hollywood's "Challenge of the Stars". *Frank Edwards, Fotos International*

"He's brought more serenity and more calmness into my life," says Jackie of steady date, actor Dennis Cole. But don't start ringing wedding bells yet. *Nate Cutler, Globe*

One of Jackie's first guest appearances (before Angels) was with Dennis Weaver on "McCloud". It certainly led to bigger and better things! *Frank Edwards, Fotos International*

Cheryl's got a winning smile and golden locks so beautiful, Wella has chosen her to be their new spokeswoman for their instant hair conditioner. *UPI*

The Ladds adore their three-year-old daughter, Jordan, and are trying everything to protect her from too much publicity and public attention. *Phil Roach, Photoreporters*

Even in 1969, no one would have called Farrah anything but gorgeous, no matter how she wore her hair. Just ask old beau Tommy Smothers! *Frank Edwards, Fotos International*

The hair was there, but different, and the teeth not quite as dazzling,when Farrah made "Inside O.U.T." for TV in 1971. Quite a change! *Wide World*

Farrah's parents, Jim and Pauline Fawcett, are prouder than punch of their baby girl. So's Farrah's nephew, Jeff Walls, sister Diane's son. *Sue Terry, Globe*

Despite their ups and downs, Lee and Farrah manage a night out every once in a while, and always have a beaming smile for the photographers. *Sylvia Norris, Photo Trends*

Right now, because they're both so busy with their careers, Lee's son from his first marriage, Lee, Jr., is enough family for the Majors.' *Phil Roach, Photoreporters*

While Farrah was in New York, without Lee, to do her new movie, she partied with Shirley MacLaine after the premiere of Shirl's "The Turning Point". *Tim Boxer, Pictorial Parade*

1977 was a very good year for Lindsay. She won an Emmy as the best actress in a dramatic series. And then ABC cancelled the show! *Wide World*

The bionic love affair between Lindsay and Lee Majors was for show only. Off-screen, the sparks flew and tempers were often shorted out. *Max Miller, Fotos International*

Michael is Lindsay's tower of power. His strength and understanding calm her down when the pressures of fame and fortune start to get to her. *Max Miller, Fotos International*

Stepping lively at the 1972 Miss World finals in London. Lynda is fourth from the left, all smiles even though she didn't win the title. *UPI*

Bullets fly off the silver bracelets at her wrists, and Wonder Woman, once again, saves the world from another villainous threat to mankind. *Photoreporters*

The traditional cake-cutting ceremony at Lynda and Ron's wedding. It was the only part of it that didn't have a Mexican flavor. *Gene Trindl, Globe*

The wedding was purposely kept small—no circus atmosphere for the Samuels—but among the guests, Jackie Smith and Dennis Cole. *Gene Trindl, Globe*

Angie was a classic beauty right from the beginning, although, in 1959, just after signing with Warner Bros., she hadn't become a blonde yet. *Wide World*

The apple of both Angie and Burt's eyes, daughter Nikki. She's a budding gymnast, and takes her physical fitness exercises very seriously. *Phil Roach, Photoreporters*

The Bacharachs are still separated, but no divorce plans have been announced. Friends still hope that they will work things out and reconcile. *Photo Trends*

Chapter 5
Jackie Smith

Of all the Angels, Jaclyn Smith is the hardest to know. She's quiet, reserved, and very much into her own thing. . .though as Kelly Garrett she's the most streetwise of the astral trio. On location, she acted as sort of a buffer between the flamboyance of Farrah and intellectualism of Kate. She is less the cushion with the addition of the eager, but inexperienced, Cheryl Ladd. The three, now, are very separate personalities, easily distinguishable in temperament from one another (much more so than at the start of the series), but Jackie is still the least outgoing of the three.

That doesn't stop her from speaking out when she feels she has been wronged, however. She says, rather vehemently, that the magazine report of her getting the role of Kelly because she was dating Rich Husky, former "Angels" producer at the time the show was being cast, was an outright lie. "I auditioned with droves of pretty girls," she says indignantly, "and they had seen me on "Switch." That helped a lot."

Actually, Jackie's beautiful face had been seen on TV in a variety of guest appearances— "McCloud," "Get Christy Love," "The Rookies" (although not with Kate), and a Disney made-for-TV film. But it was a long, hard road for the gentle miss from her comfortable, secure, Houston home to Hollywood and "Charlie's Angels."

October 26, 1945, Jaclyn Smith was born to "the sweetest people in the world," Margaret Ellen and Jack Smith. She was their second child and the first daugher (Jackie's brother, Tommy, is married and has three sons; the whole family still lives in Houston, where her dad, semi-retired, is a dentist). They always have been, and still are, a very close-knit family. It was a solid, loving, middle-class background, and Jaclyn's parents unselfishly supported every decision she made. They still do, and the family is her greatest source of security. "I still call them when I have problems," Jackie admits. "They always have the answers. People pay psychiatrists a lot of money for answers. I get mine free, and they're always the right ones." They're her best friends in the world, her parents and relatives in the Houston area, and she misses them terribly, as she does the slow, even pace of Houston life. When she goes home for a visit, she can truly relax and be herself, and reminisce about her happy, loving childhood.

Jackie took her first ballet lesson when she was three years old and her folks gave her a pair of pink satin ballet slippers. For a long time it was the path she followed. To be a prima ballerina in the great tradition of Margot Fonteyn or Maria Tallchief was her dream. The long hours of disciplined practice and afternoons of lessons made her early years lonely but not unhappy ones. She was always at the *barre* while other kids her age were out playing house or hide and seek. She never developed the knack of making friends easily.

At Pershing Junior High, and later at Lamar High School, Jackie began to expand her talents a little. She started performing with the Houston Community Playhouse and building up an impressive list of acting credits in school and little theatre productions. The stage was really the only place where Jackie lost her shyness and let her natural grace and charm emerge without the painful self-consciousness she usually experienced with her schoolmates. She was not much for group activities, and when she was forced to go to school dances she usually sat by herself, wishing she were somewhere else. "I was strictly a wallflower," Jaclyn says, "although my mother would never admit it. But the fact is I didn't relate well in school. Ballet was the only thing that occupied my mind."

Jackie didn't really fare much better at Trinity University in San Antonio, where she went to study drama and psychology. A year was all it took to make her realize how homesick and unhappy she was all the time. Again, as she had in high school, she just kept thinking about dancing. "I studied hard and I was very self-disciplined," she remembers. "I'd sit at my desk, day after day, studying all the time, and still make only C's. It sounds as though I'm not very smart...but my mind just wasn't there, even though I punished myself. I wasn't a typical co-ed. I never took part in after-school activities."

You might imagine that Jackie went home to Houston at this point, to the comfort and understanding of her loving family. She didn't. Instead, she headed straight for New York and ballet lessons with the master of dance, George Ballanchine. The rigorous practice sessions and demanding class hours forced Jackie to admit that she really didn't have the *emotional* dedication to devote her life to the ballet. The very difficult life requires enormous discipline and sacrifice, and there are very few who can so totally give up the outside world to dedicate themselves to the dance.

Jackie switched over to musical comedy, a still demanding but much less strenuous dance form. She was encouraged by friend and choreographer, Peter Genaro. She also, of course, had the encouragement of her family, emotionally and financially. "I had my Daddy," Jackie says, "so I never really struggled financially. I'm lucky. He told me not to worry about dropping out of college. 'You'll get the rest of your education living in New York' he told me, and he was right. I used to go to the opera and frequently the ballet."

Blessed with supportive parents and never having to worry about paying the rent or where her next meal was coming from (Jack Smith sent her a very generous $1,000 a month allowance), Jackie was able to get—and accept—low paying jobs in summer stock and off-off-Broadway productions.

She almost made it to Broadway twice, once in a musical based on "Peg O' My Heart," with Eartha Kitt, which closed before it ever got out of New Haven, and a second time as part of the chorus of long-legged beauties in "Gypsy." It was when this last break didn't happen that Jackie remembered a man she had met while she was doing a musical in Central Park. He was an agent for actors in TV commercials, and Jackie's lithe, green-eyed beauty caught his attention immediately. He thought she'd be perfect for TV. She wasn't quite so sure, at least not at that moment, and filed away his card for possible future use.

When the part in "Gypsy" fell through, Jackie decided the time was right, and she gave him a call. He sent her out on an interview almost immediately, and she landed her first commercial, for Listerine, with amazing ease. But it wasn't such a snap, after all. The offers didn't follow fast and furiously, and Jackie existed on money from home until they did. First Diet-Rite, then Camay Soap. Soon everyone wanted Jackie's gorgeous face selling their stuff. She became a Breck girl and switched to Wella Balsam (like another Angel). She also made commercials for Max Factor. She was living in the Barbizon Hotel for Women and quietly raking in the bucks from her TV ads. She still does, as a matter of fact, but no longer on a freelance basis. She now works for just a couple of major clients, Max Factor and Wella among them, by contract, for a hefty but pre-set fee. It cancels out the residuals, but as Jackie says, "It makes you feel awfully secure." She doesn't like to call what she was doing "modeling," but rather, "acting." "I never considered myself a model because I rarely did print. All my work was on TV. I don't think modeling prepares a woman for acting, it's too artificial. You have to pose all that time. As an actress, you must be free and natural."

There's a fine line, there, somewhere, between the two. And whatever you want to call it, Jackie was incredibly good at it. It was during this period of activity that she met Roger Davis. He was a model/actor, too, and he saw her first in the reception room of an ad agency while they were both waiting for assignments. He made up some excuse to be introduced to her, and it didn't take very long before they were a steady twosome. He proposed on their second date and in 1971 they were married; he was the first man in her life. Roger was a regular on "Dark Shadows" by then, and Jackie was perfectly content to be basically a wife, with an occasional commercial thrown in for good measure. She loved living in New York, that "living, vibrant city" as she calls it, and she loved doing the kinds of things young married New Yorkers take for granted: picnicking in Central Park; biking around the city; going to the theatre, the opera, the ballet.

It lasted only two years. Roger was offered the lead in "Alias Smith and Jones," which he naturally accepted. It was, of course, shot in Hollywood, and Jackie commuted back and forth between Roger in L.A. and her jobs in New York. The pace was hectic and enervating, and whether or not it was really Hollywood that broke their marriage up the fact is that shortly after Roger started filming the series they did separate. Neither one chooses to discuss their marriage, even now, and their divorce was finalized in 1976. (It took Jackie two years to tell her parents about it!) Jackie lives in the house she and Roger bought while they were married. They hardly lived in it and mostly rented it out, but after the divorce Jackie moved in and starting doing it over.

The break-up is a painful topic for Jackie, though she will admit that she learned how to be "emotionally independent, my own woman" and not give that up for any person. "In marriage," she reflects, "you can get to a point where you depend on a man for every little thing. Now I'm making my own decisions, even scraping my own floors and repairing my own walls. It's wonderful."

She's been remodeling the house for well over a year now, and it still isn't near done. Jackie is a perfectionist, and everything that goes into her home must be exactly right for the mood and atmosphere she is trying to create. The house, inside especially, has been compared to Tara, Scarlett O'Hara's plantation in "Gone With The Wind." Jackie is, after all, one of the most charming examples of a Southern Belle, gracious, old-fashioned, with excellent, elegant taste. She has been filling the inside of her home with the antiques she has such a fondness for, and it's taking so long to complete because Jackie insists on doing it all herself. She tried letting someone else do the legwork and scout around for her first, but it didn't work out. Taste is a very individual and personal thing, and

Jackie's is very well-defined. She likes 18th century French and English furniture, as well as the American antiques she has collected, because she likes the feeling of going back in time when she walks in her front door. "I love the era of American history when people were mannerly, when women were delicate, when things were elegant," she enthuses. "I want my house to be cozy and quaint. And I don't mind if a room is cluttered if each thing is a memory. I've collected things for a long time. One bed in the middle bedroom was mine as a little girl. I don't like a decorator look, rather things you have gotten over the years. Each thing should be a part of your life."

If she ever wanted to give up acting for interior decorating, Jackie would be a natural. She has an exquisite sense of the past and an uncanny knack for putting things together just right. She admits that sometimes she'll sit in a friend's house and mentally redecorate the room she's in. Of course, she knows that not everyone would want to live surrounded by the past, but Jackie likes it that way. She has been very lucky with her selections, too. A beautiful double brass bed she bought in New York and had shipped to California brought her double what she paid for it when she brought it to an antiques shop (she bought a queen-sized bed instead, and it is the center of attraction in her quietly lovely bedroom). Another antiques dealer offered to buy practically every piece in her house when he came to deliver something Jackie had bought.

The house is feminine, but not frilly and ruffled.

She has used vibrant greens and blues downstairs, and softer, deeper shades in the upstairs bedrooms. She just recently bought the vacant lot next door so her two dogs, Albert, a standard black French poodle, and a second pooch, of undetermined heritage and as yet unnamed, could run and exercise when she doesn't have the time to take them to the beach.

Jackie could easily turn into a stage mother. Albert is often with her when she goes on location, and has made a few guest appearances on "Charlie's Angels." (His TV debut, in fact, prompted Kate Jackson to bring her Husky, Catcher, along, and Farrah to bring one of her several canines to work. The competition for dog guest shots got so fierce that after a while the producers decided to use only professionals.) "He got me so nervous in one scene," Jackie says about her almost-star dog, "that I kept fluffing my lines. I was worried that he was under too much stress, and so when it came to the word 'horse,' I kept saying 'hoss' in my Texas accent. They had to shoot it several times until I got it right." Nonetheless, Albert and Jackie got through it alright. He's a big, lovable dog, who obviously adores his mistress, and vice-versa. Jackie sometimes wishes she could find a man with a disposition as sweet.

There are certainly men in Jackie's life; whether they are quite so endearing as Albert, only Jackie knows for sure. One frequent date is Dennis Cole, who you've seen in TV series like "The Felony Squad," and "Bracken's World." They met on the set of "Charlie's Angels"—Dennis had a guest role

—but his scenes were mostly with Farrah and Kate. A mutual friend told him to say hello to Jackie while he was there, since they were both Texans and obviously had a lot in common. "I was smitten at first sight," says Dennis. "Not only is she one of the most beautiful girls I have known, but she is beautiful inside, too. I'm really crazy about her."

Early in 1977, they were together at the March of Dimes Ball in Houston. Although the ballroom was filled with 12,000 people, it was Dennis and Jackie who stood out. They danced the evening away, and then Jackie took Dennis home to meet her parents—that's the old-fashioned kind of girl she is, you know, one who still likes her family to meet her dates when it's possible. They liked the handsome, charming young actor, and he liked them, too.

They turned up together at one of Hollywood's biggest parties in April, holding hands and being especially loving. They were in Las Vegas together for the Jimmy Connors/Ilie Nastase tennis match in the Spring, and were photographed quite often out to dinner, or at some function or another, throughout the rest of 1977.

But close friends of Jackie's say that although she and Dennis might date, her heart really belongs to Alan Austin, owner of an exclusive ladies' clothing shop in Los Angeles. Jackie will go as far as admitting there *is* a special man in her life, she won't reveal *who* he is. What she will reveal is a fervent wish to get married again and raise a houseful of children.

"I'm dying to have kids," she says earnestly. "A lot, if I can. But realistically, I'm wondering when I'm going to get started. You can't rush into a marriage just for the sake of being married. I'd like to meet someone who thinks the way I do, but it isn't easy." Jackie admitted this a little ruefully. Her very high standards are difficult for any man to meet. She wants a man who is intelligent, understanding, perceptive, generous, strong, etc. He must be loving and love children and animals as Jackie does. And he must have a strong feeling for family. That's very important to Ms. Smith.

Another actor would be okay with her, as long as they were both working—hopefully on the same time schedules. It can be extremely hard on a show business marriage if one partner is working steadily and the other isn't, or if their commitments are so diverse they hardly get to see each other. "I'm looking for a soulmate, not a roommate," Jackie explains. "It's funny. I used to think that because I came from an ideal background, it would be so simple to get married and settle down. Now I realize that a lot of things go into a marriage."

She does think, often, that if she can't find herself a suitable husband in a year or two she'd certainly consider adopting a child. Being a single parent is a difficult job, but Jackie adores children and, fortunately, has the financial resources to draw on should she choose to adopt. She has always dreamed of teaching ballet to children, and during her early days in New York she helped to set up a Head Start ballet program for underprivileged kids. It was one of the happiest times in her life. As she says, "The deeper pleasures in life are concentrating on someone else." Jackie tried to become a "Big Sister," but was turned down by the organization. At first she didn't quite understand the rejection and was, in fact, insulted by it. But she realized that her love for children, and all she could give to them, wouldn't make up for her lack of time because of the demanding schedule of the show. This, of course, would be a very real consideration for her to deal with if she ever decided to adopt a child. Being a single, working mother would add an extra burden to the relationship between parent and child, and it would probably be a factor not in her favor if she did decide to do it. Meanwhile, though, Jackie spends a good deal of her vacation time teaching ballet to asthmatic children. It is very rewarding and gives her a sense of fulfillment. It's her own way of saying "thank you" for her own wonderful childhood.

One of Jackie's other vacation pursuits is coming to New York to go to the ballet and shop. New York, to many people, doesn't sound like the ideal vacation spot, but Los Angeles, with all its many attractions, doesn't get that much first-rate dance. And to a balletophile like Jackie, New York has the best there is to be seen. She almost got to meet one of her ballet idols in California, Mikhail Baryshnikov, who was filming "The Turning Point," with Shirley MacClaine and Anne Bancroft for Twentieth Century-Fox. Jackie was able to wangle a special permit to get on the set. Unfortunately, when Jackie was able to break away from filming on "Angels," Baryshnikov was on location elsewhere. So she never did manage to see him. And the last time she was in New York, he was out on the coast filming.

Her trip wasn't a total loss, though. She managed to get to Henri Bendel, Bonwit's, Bergdorf's, and all the best Manhattan shops. She is friendly and far prettier in person and never hesitates for a minute to sign autographs, even when she is in the midst of a purchase. "I'm a big shopper," Jackie laughs. "It's a sad, sad story. A lot of times, when I go into a store, I'll have something in mind. But a lot of times it's just luck."

Her tastes are usually classic—blazers and well-tailored pants or skirts, beautiful silk blouses with floppy bows, lace, lovely feminine things, antique jewelry. She buys a lot of clothes, but she's not really extravagant with them. They are timeless rather than trendy, and she can—and does—wear them for years. She gets to keep some of the things she wears on the show, so she often chooses them herself to make sure Kelly has that distinctive look that reflects Jackie's own personal tastes.

Her real extravagances are mostly centered on her house and her Jaguar X16, and she admits, lapsing into a Texas drawl, "Believe me, I like makin' money because I like spendin' it. I've spent most of my money, I admit."

It embarrasses Jackie to talk about either how much she makes (estimates run high: in 1977 she'll probably rake in more than $1 million from her salary, TV movies, and residuals—triple what it was last year) or how much she spends.* She grew up in a household where money was not a topic of conversation. She never knew how much her father made, and like most well-bred Southern girls she never asked. She never lacked for anything, but was taught never to take money for granted, either. "In this business, you can make fantastic amounts of money in a day, but at times it really is pennies from heaven," Jackie says a touch reluctantly. "We have tremendous pressures and very long hours, so I feel I deserve what I'm making now. But then I see a struggling intern working the same kinds of hours, and I think there's no need to talk about it so much because he's certainly not making the same kind of salary."

So money is a taboo subject with Jackie, but what she does to earn it certainly is not. She loves to talk about "Charlie's Angels" and the way it has changed her life.

Jackie's up early every morning to be ready by 5:30 when a limousine picks her up to take her to the studio. Once there, Jackie has an enormous breakfast—bacon, eggs, blueberry muffins, pancakes: the works. The thought of that much food at

*She just signed a three million dollar deal with ABC to form her own production company, GH Productions (named for her grandfather), to bring back the old, romantic movies she's always loved; tender, sweet stories like "The Last Time I Saw Paris". She's also invested several million dollars in real estate. She's not just beautiful, she's smart, too.

that hour of the morning could make a truck driver nauseous, but not Jackie. She had this eye-opening meal written into her new contract. "I need three squares a day, and breakfast is the most important meal of them all for me. If I don't have a good breakfast, I die."

Nutritionists would agree that a hearty breakfast is the proper way to start the day. And Jackie works it all off in nervous energy, so she never has to diet. In fact, she has her trouble gaining weight. The series is very physical: once Farrah threw her over her shoulder and Jackie landed so hard she bounced. Between 15 hour work days, running with the dogs, and the strenuous ballet exercises she practices at home each night, Jackie doesn't have to watch her calories—even after occasional binges on Mexican food or pizza.

Surprisingly, Jackie doesn't think she's either beautiful or well-proportioned. "I don't look good in a bikini. I've got skinny bowlegs. And all men don't think I'm beautiful, and all women certainly don't. Not everyone likes my type. And I'm not in Raquel Welch's league—anyone can see that. . . . I really have to laugh at all the fuss . . . there are millions of beautiful girls around."

Well, keep on laughing, Jackie. Ugly women rarely make the covers of the top magazines in the country—she recently turned down offers from two of the most prominent magazines in the country. Jackie's a very morally concerned individual, "old-fashioned and conservative" she calls it. She doesn't smoke or drink, and "heck" is about the strongest word in her vocabulary. She doesn't care for most of the films being made today and would choose very carefully before accepting any offers. She proudly sticks to the values handed down to her from her grandfather, a Methodist minister, and her grandmother, with whom she was very close (her grandmother died at age 101 about a year ago). They were the strongest influences in her life and represent exactly what she wants for herself in the future.

"I once read somewhere that conscience is God's presence in man," Jackie says. "I believe that. I have an overactive conscience, and I can't do one bad thing." Even when she was in college, and missed a class, her whole day was ruined. Her father used to tell her, "forget it, don't take it so seriously." But she did. Even now, grown up as she is, when she's "bad" her conscience won't let her forget it. Jackie laughs at herself, but she means it, every word. She has turned down movie roles that meant appearing in the nude and even took a smaller role than the one she was originally offered in the film version of "The Adventurers" because when she signed the contract she never imagined there would be a nude scene for her in the movie. There was. And she categorically refused to do it. "That's only for the person I love and no one else," says Jackie. "What you give the person you love is yourself, and it's not for millions to see. That's my upbringing talking again. I don't care if it's an Academy Award film, if it requires me to do nudity or has subject matter I don't approve of, I won't do it. I want to appear in pictures I can be proud of."

Due to her conservative beliefs her film career could easily be limited to Disney epics and made-for-TV movies like the one she completed last summer while she was on hiatus from "Angels." It's a Western, with Mitchell Ryan and Michael Parks, and Jackie's character is as pure as the driven snow.

Whether it's modesty, good old-fashioned shyness, or just a severe case of the goody-two-shoes, Jackie admits she's "out of sync" with the morals and manners of Hollywood. And if you look at the way she spends her time, you'll see that it's true. No swinging party life—although she does go to some big Hollywood functions, especially network ones—she'd much rather stay home with the dogs, a good book, or a few close friends. She likes those quiet times when she can curl up and fall asleep while reading—they're peaceful and relaxing, as are her hours in the park, just walking, or taking a long, leisurely drive into the nearby mountains. Unfortunately, those times are all too few. The series is demanding, and it has taken its toll on Jackie and the other Angels.

"You tend not to have a life of your own. You come home, eat dinner, study your lines, and go to sleep." That's not truly a complaint, merely a fact of the life of an Angel. "I just like to go home and drop everything," Jackie says. "I don't like to talk on the phone, and I have to watch myself sometimes from getting rude. It's just that I'm so tired and want some peace and quiet and a complete departure from what I have been doing."

What she's been doing for 12-15 hours each day is being Kelly Garrett, the Angel with the quiet manner and the one destined to be the real center of attraction now that Farrah's gone. It was never intended for any of the Angels to be the singular star of the show. Sabrina, it's true, is the nominal leader, but all three were created equal. According to Jackie, and Kate Jackson certainly agrees, in the beginning the show was sleek and glib and you could hardly tell the characters apart, except physically. Slowly, the scripts individualized the three Angels, and the actresses themselves brought their own styles and interpretations to their roles.

Jackie was upset when Farrah upped and left. The three girls had been incredibly friendly and supportive of each other. As Jackie says, "It might sound crazy to say, but I enjoyed working with Farrah and Kate. We started out as strangers, but real warmth and fondness grew up between us."

Jackie was also aware that should the series end because of the absent Angel, she could have been out of a job. She's the first one to tell you she's not a great actress, but she's learning all the time. And if nothing else, "Charlie's Angels" is the best "on-the-job" training any young actress could ask for. Fortunately, although the legal hassles have yet to be resolved, the Angels go on solving crimes and saving innocent lives, and Cheryl Ladd has fit right into the group. They all have contracts that now have a "favored nations" clause—whatever one gets, they all get—other than salary, naturally. It makes things easier for everybody.

All the Angels have defended the show against

the almost boring, by now, charges of its being sexist. Here's Jackie's thoughts on the matter: "It's not true at all. The show has to be more than three pretty faces flitting around. The way I see it is that we are three different types who happen to blend together very well. Nobody claims the show is intellectual. It's just a big fun fantasy thing, and people apparently want light entertainment at night."

She sounds amazingly like Kate Jackson on the subject; maybe because a fast on-set friendship has grown up between them—they have the same hairdresser, and they're both unmarried at the moment. And Kate sort of protects Jackie, especially when she needs it most. One day when Jackie's call was much earlier than necessary, it was Kate who made the producers apologize and promise to be more considerate in the future. Yet it's really just on the set that they are so friendly, since neither of them has the time to develop it more socially. Besides, though Jackie says Kate is the best driver on the show, she finds it a little "scary" to be with her. Apparently, the exuberant Ms. Jackson likes to keep her foot on the gas pedal all the time, and quite to the discomfort of the conservative Ms. Smith.

She is surprised but delighted with the easy way the show—with Cheryl Ladd—has eased itself into the new season. She was equally ecstatic the first year. "I was hoping the show would be accepted, but I had no idea it would be among the nation's top 5 programs! And then there's the fan mail. It comes from all over. Surprisingly, a lot of women write to me, and some want photos to give to their husbands. I know I wouldn't do anything like that if I were married. One lady asked me for a picture so she could give it to her husband on his birthday. Now isn't that wild?" It is if you're Jaclyn Smith, whose beauty would probably preclude her husband ever asking for a picture of someone else.

Being an actress means a lot to Jackie, although she's not overly ambitious. She wants to be a better actress, naturally, but she feels she has other resources to draw from, especially her family. Their warmth and unpretentiousness has kept her from losing her perspective. She says, without a trace of self-consciousness, "I don't have the need to surround myself all the time with all the trappings of being a big star. If my mother and daddy love me, and one other person, I'm happy. I was happy before 'Charlie's Angels,' I'm happy now, and if it stopped tomorrow, I'd still be happy."

Chapter 6
Cheryl Ladd

Cheryl Ladd is not just the newest Angel, she's the littlest, the youngest, and the only one of them who's married and a mother.

She walked into a situation where someone older and wiser might have "feared to tread," but you don't just turn down the biggest break of your career just because you're scared silly that the ghost of your predecessor will be haunting the set and the minds of the public. Not if you're Cheryl, you don't.

When Farrah Fawcett-Majors announced she was not going to return to "Charlie's Angels," knees started knocking all over the place. If "Angels" had any one specific thing going for it, Farrah was it. In principle, the show had no real star, but in reality more attention was paid to Farrah, her hair and her teeth, than anything else the news media could possibly focus on. Could there be a show without her? Was she really serious? No one knew either answer, but no one wanted to take any chances.

So Cheryl Ladd was hired as Angel number four. If Farrah came back, all well and good, Cheryl, as Kris Munroe, would just play younger sister to Farrah's Jill. If she didn't, Kris would assume her place as number three.

The tension on the set the first day was incredible. It was hoped that hiring Cheryl would scare Farrah into returning to the show, and everybody was waiting. The script included her, but, if necessary, they could shoot around her for a while and write the character out completely if they needed to. Cheryl was nervous. She had a job, but it was on the line. If Farrah didn't show up, would they really go on as if she had never been on the show at all? Or was it just a ploy to force Farrah into living up to the terms of her contract?

It became very obvious, after a short while, that Farrah was not going to set foot on the set of "Charlie's Angels" that day, or probably any day. She actually wasn't even in the country; she and Lee had flown to Iran for a vacation. So they shot around her. When it was apparent to all concerned that Farrah was indeed, and irrevocably, a fallen angel, shooting was resumed. With the help of an understanding husband and an empathetic group of co-stars, Cheryl was welcomed into the fold.

She's been around the business awhile. Her first real acting part was as the voice of the cat in the cartoon movie, "Josie and the Pussycat." From there it was on to over 100 commercials for such varied products as Ford Thunderbird, Michelob

Beer, Prell Shampoo, Johnson and Johnson Baby Powder, and Ultra-Brite toothpaste. And everything from walk-ons to one liners in "The Rookies," "Ironside," "Switch," and "Police Woman."

But it was her first feature film, "Jamaica Reef," that really changed her life. It didn't quite get her career into high gear—the movie was an unqualified bomb—but she did meet her husband, David Ladd, on location shooting in the Caribbean. It was definitely *not* love at first sight, however.

David's father was the late actor, Alan Ladd, and his mother, Sue, is a respected agent. Older brother, Alan Ladd, Jr., is head of Twentieth Century-Fox and the man who brought you "Star Wars." It's a totally show biz family. David was in the process of divorcing his first wife and was, at the time, as Cheryl says, "not very together. We fought about everything. It was insane. Like World War III. We were hostile because we had both just been through difficult relationships. We were very nervous about getting hurt again. But we did the right thing; we just became friends first. We went back to Hollywood together and things developed after a few dinners out."

What developed was a meeting with David's mom, who adored Cheryl on sight, and then a wedding, in 1973, in Las Vegas. David's brother was best man, and Cheryl's parents, Marion and Dolores Stoppelmoor, watched tearfully, but happily, as their beautiful daughter said "I do."

Cheryl is the only one of the Angels who is not

a Southern Belle, although she could easily pass, if she wanted to. She was born in Huron, South Dakota, on July 12, 1951; the second oldest of four children.

Before Cheryl's climb to star status, Huron was a quiet little town with tree-shaded streets and fine looking old houses. It's only other claim to fame was being the birthplace of Hubert Humphrey. The Stoppelmoors still live there: Marion is an engineer for the Chicago and Northwestern Railroad; Dolores, a former waitress, is a happy, contented housewife. They met when he was 19 and she was 16. "It was love at first sight," Cheryl says of her parents' first meeting. Cheryl and David want to experience that same kind of satisfaction and fulfillment in their own marriage.

Cheryl grew up fast. Of all her friends and family only her mother had complete faith in—or at least could tolerate—Cheryl's potential for fulfilling her wildest dream: becoming a movie star. Everyone else kind of hoped she'd outgrow it, but her mom haunted rummage sales and bargain counters for clothes for Cheryl to dress up in and play make-believe. At age six, when all the other little girls in the neighborhood were playing house and mothering their dolls, Cheryl was using the front of the Stoppelmoor house to stage musicals and skits. She knew, even then, that some day she'd make it to Hollywood. "I was the Otto Preminger of my block," she laughs now, and by age 8 she was taking singing and dancing lessons, not always the easiest things for her family to afford to give her.

"They didn't have a dime," she says of her

family's early financial problems. "I was musical as a kid and begged them for a piano, but they couldn't afford one. I danced and sang before I could talk. I lived a fantasy life. My sister was good at cooking and sewing, but I wasn't. I *had* to be a ham." Somehow, money was found, and if Cheryl didn't have her piano, at least she had her lessons.

She became a cheerleader in high school and sang with a local band called the Music Shop. When she graduated from Huron High, in 1969, she joined the band on the road and crisscrossed the country doing one-nighters in towns that made Huron, with its population of 15,000, look like a huge metropolis. Though she says the experience gave her a lot of poise, she thought she was just awful, and she dismisses the whole thing with a giggle. "The band was going on tour and looking for a girl singer. They must have been desperate, that's why I got the job. I learned thirty-five songs in a week-and-a-half, all except the bottom five of the Top 40. On weekends they replaced me with a bellydancer. We began the tour in a steakhouse in Iowa, and things didn't get any better. The band wound up in Thousand Oaks, California. When they broke up, I went to Los Angeles."

That's Cheryl's side of the story, and a pretty grim self-appraisal of her musical talents. But the leader of the group, Doug Almond, who is now a Huron College music professor, remembers it all a little differently and thinks Cheryl had a big role in the group's successes. He found Cheryl through a mutual friend who had heard her sing at talent shows, and Doug was duly impressed. "She had tremendous moxie for a young girl," he said. "She could really hold an audience. We started to mold the whole group to showcase Cherie."

Doug says that the group broke up, not because they weren't good, but because, by mutual agreement, the guys in the band decided it was time for them to settle down, get married, and have families. And time, too, for Cheryl to get a serious start on her Hollywood career. It hardly makes a difference whose version is the absolute truth. Obviously a future in singing was not what Cheryl really wanted anyway. She wanted to be a movie star.

It wasn't easy. Cheryl did nothing during those first few years that was particularly noteworthy. She didn't even get chased around a desk by a casting director, something her mom, in weekly phone calls, kept warning her to avoid like the plague. "My dumb cheerleader routine kept them away," Cheryl says with a twinkle in her baby blues. "If someone would suggest something, I'd giggle in a dinkly little voice, "Oh, gee, I don't think I'd really better do that. By the time I got through, he didn't think so either."

So Cheryl managed to preserve her virtue, or at least her principles anyway, as she made countless 30-second appearances in a bathing suit introducing emcees and welcoming audiences to this show or that. But it began to get to her after a while, and she even thought about giving up her dream—although what she'd do then was a question she never satisfactorily answered.

"I had seven years of things you'd forget as

soon as you saw them," Cheryl says reflectively. "Then something happened that crushed me completely. I wanted desperately to play the daughter in the 'Family' series. After seven days of readings in the producers' office, it came down to just me and Meredith Baxter-Birney. God! Then she got it. I wish her well, but I can tell you, I was heartbroken. Not even David could calm me."

If Cheryl had been a little less committed to acting, or less serious about developing a real career, a blow like that could easily have been just the right excuse to give it all up. It was almost an attractive possibility to stay home and be the kind of wife and mother David really would like her to be. She had told him, long before, that she would do that if he really wanted her to, but that, ultimately, he would be unhappy with the results.

"You fell in love with someone who works and has something going for herself with a life and a passion of her own," Cheryl told David. "When that passion is gone, I'll be a different person." She had laid it on the line this time, and they talked about it a lot and thought about it a lot, and finally Cheryl called her agent and told him she wanted to work. She would have given up her career if David had asked her to—"I'd do anything for him," she insists—but luckily for everyone, David didn't. He is an understanding and perceptive man, no stranger himself to the ups and downs of the life of an actor dedicated to his career. His own father was able to combine family and profession without too much strain on either. And, fortunately, David is the kind of person who has been easily able to handle Cheryl's sudden rise to fame while his own career has been, at best, steady, rather than sensational. He has had the good, meaty kinds of roles that looked as if they just might push him to the top, when Cheryl was just plowing through walk-ons, virtually unknown and unnoticed. "It just happens that Cheryl got her series first," he says. "She worked hard for her chance, it wasn't just handed to her, and I'm working for mine." With a mischievous grin, David adds, "When somebody in my family *isn't* famous, then I start to worry."

They have a lovely kind of relationship that allows them to celebrate each other's successes with total enjoyment and no jealousy. The main thing is that they are both working constantly. David is busy in television all the time; Cheryl with the series. They are just not competitive professionally, and that acts as a stronger bond than almost anything else. If not for David's steady, supportive personality, Cheryl might not have decided to accept the role of Kris Munroe in "Charlie's Angels."

She was considering a couple of different offers when Aaron Spelling called. He had seen her in a small part on "The Rookies," and remembered her reading for "Family." She was crazy with excitement when Spelling told her she had the part, but she wasn't sure. Did she really want it? Could she really do it? What about Farrah? "It was the thought of dealing with the rejection, if in fact it would happen . . . the idea of stepping into those shoes . . . ." Cheryl remembers her dilemma as if it were yesterday. "I didn't know if I could handle it.

Wondering if there was going to be any resentment, not necessarily from the cast, but from the public. But I don't know Farrah, and I have my own role now. The character is developed."

David was right behind her, a pillar of strength, urging her on, boosting her confidence, knowing that she could do whatever she set her mind to do. It was David who faced the press and told them, in no uncertain terms, that Cheryl was not going to be a carbon copy of Farrah, she was going to be her own person.

Originally the character of Kris Munroe was developed as Jill's sister, so in case Farrah didn't return to the series, as happened, there would still be three Angels. Kris/Cheryl made her debut on September 14, 1977—without Farrah. And although that first, two-hour episode did not go smoothly, it did cement a good, solid relationship among the three stars. "It was rough," Cheryl admits about the first weeks on the set with Jaclyn Smith and Kate Jackson. "We were testing each other. Luckily, we shared the same dressing room, and you can get pretty close under those conditions. I know Kate and Jaclyn were very upset when Farrah left. When someone you worked closely with jeopardizes your livelihood, you can't help but resent it a little bit."

It wasn't just Jackie and Kate who were upset. David Doyle, the patriarchal Bosley, was shattered, to say the least. He's a seasoned actor: he played Bridget's father in "Bridget Loves Bernie," and Dick Van Dyke's boss on his show. He has starred on Broadway and in the movies. But if

"Charlie's Angels" went off the air, he would be unemployed.

It didn't take very long, however, to see that Cheryl was going to be okay, and the show would go on. "Looks wise," David says, "Cheryl is just as impressive, and she's as gifted as, if not more so, than Farrah. I think it's a stronger show now."

A quick, mutual-admiration society grew up between the two of them. "Within two weeks, because of David's friendliness and warmth, we were all friends. I feel like David's my adopted Dad," Cheryl says. To which, David replies, "She was eager, a little nervous, but a pro. No one did this girl a favor by giving her a job. She can cut it, which we all knew after a couple of days of shooting."

Those are pretty fine words from an old pro like David Doyle, and Cheryl knows and appreciates it. "If anyone should act like a star," she says, "It's David Doyle. He really knows the craft the way I hope to someday, and he has real sensitivity."

But Cheryl really didn't have much to worry about. Both Kate and Jackie are resilient ladies, and it didn't take long for both of them to announce publicly that they thought Cheryl was a better actress than Farrah. Nor did Cheryl have to wait more than a couple of days for the production crew to claim, with big smiles on their faces, that they were all "really high and confident on Cheryl." She quickly became one of the gang, directing lunch-hour calisthenics classes, and offering a sympathetic shoulder to anyone who needed it. There was no question, Cheryl was as completely and quickly accepted into the folds of the "Charlie's Angels" cast and crew as she could have hoped. And as for the public, well, they adore Kris Munroe, and Cheryl, too. The ratings have not slipped an iota.

How does Cheryl view the character of Kris Munroe? She hopes to see her grow within the series and is trying desperately to make her real and believable. "She's fresh from the police academy, but she has street smarts. She has a certain vulnerability. . . she's not callous yet. I'm playing that it's an effort for her to try and be tough. She admires the other girls and looks to them for advice, watching how they handle certain situations. Kris kind of looks like, 'Oh, so that's how it's done!'"

Actually, Cheryl is playing herself to a large extent, specifically so people will be able to relate to the character. She has a zany sense of humor that she is bringing to Kris, who is not perfect and makes all kinds of mistakes. She tries the best she can and has all the best intentions in the world, but occasionally, as everyone does, she falls over her own two feet. She is sort of the comic relief, "clumsy, not too smooth," as Cheryl says, "quite different from Farrah's part."

Cheryl works very closely, whenever possible, with the show's writers, trying to make Kris more human. She'd rather give up a line, or even a scene, if she thinks it's out of character, and she is really trying hard to give everything she can to the role. By all accounts, she is succeeding. While Cheryl's fan mail is not quite up to what Farrah's was, it's growing steadily week by week. And Cheryl is happy. She likes her co-workers and the crew, "We're at the point where everybody is playing practical jokes. Everyone is so nice." And she is learning all the time.

At 5′ 3″ and 103 pounds, 26 year old Cheryl is a natural athlete—tennis, gymnastics, scuba-diving (she either looks a little like Farrah or a lot like rock singer Peter Frampton, depending on whom you ask). But for the very first show, when she had to ride a surfboard, she fell and hit her elbow so hard she was in agony for days. But since there were somewhere between 20 to 25,000 people watching the Angels film in Waikiki, Cheryl knew she'd be terribly embarrassed if she fell off again. She made it on her second try, and everybody cheered. It was, she says, "the greatest moment I've ever had in acting."

On location in Hawaii, Cheryl ran into her first and only difficulty with Farrah fans. Someone in the crowd called out during the shooting, "Where's Farrah? Up until then, I was just working hard and not dealing with that problem," Cheryl says. "Then, when he called out, I realized that out of all those thousands of people only one person had said that. I grinned a mile wide, and I'm sure my reaction wasn't understood."

Though Cheryl really loves her work, and has gone through a lot of hard times before she got to this point in her career, she won't let it be her whole life. It's important, of course, and she is ambitious, naturally, but not to the extent that her family is ever neglected. She and David have worked very hard at handling her success: it's been a total team effort. David is thrilled with her development as Kris Munroe, even though some "friends" taunted him with not so subtle hints that he might have trouble handling it all. But Cheryl is as firm as David in her philosophy. "We're not in competition with each other. We'll deal with it. We've shared and experienced it. Every decision in our household has been made by us and for us."

David cooks breakfast at 5:30 each morning and drives Cheryl to the studio. But he's not the dinner chef—Cheryl's kitchen boasts a sign that says, "Love is eating out so your husband doesn't have to cook dinner." Cheryl took off from work to help David work on his starring role in "The Glass Menagerie" in Palm Springs last summer. She helped him learn lines, went to rehearsals with him every night, and was at least as nervous as he was on opening night.

The Ladd's biggest and most constant decisions revolve around their three year old daughter, Jordan (named after the character in F. Scott Fitzgerald's "The Great Gatsby," because she had a lot of spunk). It was their concern for Jordan and her future security, Cheryl says, that drove away all their doubts when both of them were considering quitting show business altogether.

Cheryl's the strict disciplinarian of the family. She doesn't want her daughter to grow up to be a typical spoiled Hollywood brat. So, although she occasionally comes to work with mom—where there is no lack of babysitters—the Ladd's try their best to keep Jordan out of the public eye. It was a public relations person who cajoled Cheryl into bringing Jordan out during the press conference that announced Cheryl's joining of "Charlie's Angels." "I don't like Jordan to be photographed," Cheryl explains. "I'm not about to push her into the celebrity thing. She has got to be a kid first. I had a happy childhood, climbing trees, skinning my knees, playing baseball. I want that for Jordan, too."

"Cheryl's a good parent," Jaclyn Smith says, "and that's the nicest compliment I could give anyone."

Cheryl often thinks about what Jordan will be like grown up. The times and attitudes will be very different from those of Cheryl's childhood, and she hopes she'll be able to explain to her daughter why she feels the way she does about certain things. "As long as we can talk to each other, everything will be alright. That's how you keep a marriage or any relationship together. You have to be honest and talk to each other; the minute you stop, it's all over."

Cheryl's attitudes towards childrearing are greatly influenced by the way her own parents brought her up. Her dad is warm and loving—as David is with Jordan—and her mom is a whiz at anything from hanging wallpaper to reupholstering furniture. Cheryl isn't quite so handy, but their cute little white clapboard house in the Hollywood Hills—the non-celebrity part—is filled with the kinds of personal touches that show how very important home and hearth are to Cheryl and her husband.

The house itself is no mansion, but Cheryl says

she cried when she saw it because it was the kind of house she has wanted since she was a kid. It has beautiful hand-rubbed wooden floors, high beamed ceilings, and lots of mementos from David and Cheryl's travels. The focal point of the house is a wonderful antique piano that friends gather around on weekends to sing and have a good time. They usually spend very simple weekends at home, either alone, teaching Jordan to swim, or just enjoying each other's company, or with a close group of actor-friends, none of whom is rich, famous, or instantly recognizable. They prefer it that way; Cheryl whips up sandwiches and lemonade, and maybe sometimes they'll play charades or music games. It might sound boring to those used to, or expecting, the glamorous party life of the Hollywood elite. But to Cheryl and David it's fun, and what they enjoy most.

The first few months of "Charlie's Angels," while not quite putting a strain on the Ladd's solid marriage, did give them a few rough moments. Cheryl was afraid that people would be angry at her for trying to take Farrah's place. That fear, of course, turned out to be unfounded. And there was never really any problem about David's reaction. "Good, bad, or indifferent, I'll still be here," he says. "Two things that sustain us in this business are our relationship and our feeling of self-worth. Cheryl can handle both the fame and the rejection of an acting career. If you don't have a strong ego, this town can kill you."

Cheryl agrees. "You have to be prepared for acting, physically, emotionally, and mentally. As my husband says, 'Sometimes you're hot and sometimes cold.' There's ups and downs, just like life."

Right now, Cheryl is hot, and that's an understatement. Her contract allows her to do lots of other things, and she is taking full advantage of the opportunities—a guest appearance on the "Donny and Marie Show"; movies-of-the-week in which she gets to play roles totally different from Kris Munroe. She has a recording contract and would like to find the time to work an album out.

"What are my dreams?" she asks. "I want to have another child, to star in a Broadway musical, to direct a film, to write a book, to go to Europe. . . .".

Those are the dreams for a lifetime, nothing imminent, nothing for tomorrow. Right now, Cheryl is happy concentrating on today.

"I've always been a happy person. Now I have a new kind of exuberance because I'm doing something I've been waiting for so long. One of my worries is I might lose my happiness and peace of mind. I've enjoyed having a child, being married to a wonderful man, living in a wonderful house, being with close friends. I don't want to lose all that."

Chapter 7
Farrah

"Pretty girls have problems, too," Farrah Fawcett-Majors says, flashing a toothy grin. It's a little hard to feel sorry for the world's most famous hyphenate, who's not merely pretty, but gorgeous. Whatever "problems" she has can only be insignificant ones next to her startling beauty and enormous popularity.

Since she decided not to return to "Charlie's Angels" for the Fall, 1977 season, Farrah has been on the move in her usual energetic, enthusiastic fashion. Her decision came about after much careful considering and long hours of talking it over with her husband, Lee Majors.

On March 8, 1977, Farrah informed the producers of the show that she was not coming back. It wasn't the $5,000 a week salary that was bothering her, although she certainly wouldn't mind a few more dollars a week, she just wanted time to do other things, like movies. No one, especially not the producers, took her all that seriously. After all, they reasoned, someone who only got to be the household word she is through the show wouldn't just give it all up on a whim—would she?

They began to believe Farrah wasn't kidding when she and Lee decided to form Fawcett-Majors Productions, a film production company to make movies for theatrical distribution and TV. Lee put additional pressure on ABC by threatening to quit his series, "The Six Million Dollar Man," in order to pursue other interests. He was involved in filming "A Matter of Innocence" for NBC; Farrah let it be known that she was having a rough time deciding which, if any, of the forty-plus projects she'd been offered she might be interested in. . . . It might be "The Fan Club" or "Sweet Savage Love," based on Rosemary Rogers gothic bestseller.

In fact, Farrah chose first to become the spokeswoman for Fabergé, doing commercials and spending a good part of August being incredibly visible all over New York City. She was apartment hunting, with the help of her sister, Diane Fawcett Wells (who just happens to be Fabergé's southeastern United States representative), for a Manhattan residence to use when she started her first feature film since leaving the series, "Somebody Killed Her Husband." "So why should I do another season of 'Charlie's Angels' for $5,000 an episode?" Farrah asked then. "Why shouldn't I work for myself and Lee?"

The producers and ABC, amid predictions of doom, failure, and quick forgetfulness on the part of her public, took heavy action to keep her from leaving.

1. They accused her of breaking her contract, the standard five-year series type; one year down, four to go. She and Lee immediately countered with the claim that she had never even signed a contract. No excuse, they said. "She, and we, have been operating under that unsigned contract for a year, which means she has a binding contract in every sense of the word, according to legal procedure." A very large percentage of TV commitments are sealed with a verbal agreement and a handshake; they are usually considered as binding as anything signed on the dotted line.

2. They began to spread stories of Farrah's exorbitant money demands. She wanted $25,000 a show; even $100,000, and lots of time off to make her movies. It sounded as if Farrah was just another money-grubbing starlet on a monumental ripoff campaign. According to her press agent and personal manager, Jay Bernstein, "Farrah would not consider coming back for even one million dollars a show." So there! They weren't scaring her one bit.

3. ABC was understandably in an uproar. Not only was "Charlie's Angels" the most popular show on TV, but it was Farrah Fawcett-Majors who made it that. Her defection was bigger news than the opening of the baseball season. *Time* magazine reported it. TV news covered it. Everybody was taking sides. They threatened to try and legally prevent any movie company from hiring her. Farrah and Lee had the last laugh. They took off for a

little sightseeing in Iran, dropping in to visit the Shah, and gave themselves a little time and distance away from the network battles.

4. In May, while Farrah and Lee were still out of town, ABC announced that a fourth Angel, Cheryl Ladd, had been hired. She would play Kris Munroe, sister to Farrah's Jill. Nobody actually said so, and in fact, everybody, including Cheryl, denied it, but it seemed as if ABC was hedging its bets. If Farrah did not come back, Cheryl could ease right into third place. Nobody knew for sure whether Farrah's demands for more money were real or just an excuse for leaving. It didn't really matter. The big question was would there be a show or not?

June 1, the first day of shooting for the new season, and everyone was getting ready to leave for Hawaii where most of the first episode would be shot. Everyone but Farrah, that is. Contrary to all hopes and expectations, she was a no-show. Shooting was suspended, and the lawyers, the producers, and the network executives all got together to "get Farrah." Spelling-Goldberg was already suing her for breach of contract; ABC chimed in with a huge suit for damages and an injunction against her working in any other series or film. At that point, with twenty-six episodes to be filmed and only half of one done, it truly looked as if there would be no "Charlie's Angels" in the Fall. An awful lot hung on Farrah: jobs, money, ratings. This was no joke and ABC was taking it very seriously. The end of the Angels could mean the end of ABC's reign as the #1 network in the country. It was too much to lose.

"I can't be happy playing someone who never cries, always smiles, and never shows any real emotion," were Farrah's parting words. Cheryl Ladd was only too happy to keep on smiling, and even if she hadn't been, the producers were being deluged with letters and photographs of hopeful beauties who thought they filled the necessary requirements of beauty, good figure and gorgeous hair.

Cheryl easily fit all those requirements, except for the haircut, but she does just fine without it.

Don't imagine for a minute that merely because "Charlie's Angels" is a number one smash this season without Farrah the producers have let their lawsuit against her just fade away. They still hadn't decided whether or not to ask for an injunction to keep her from starting Martin Poll's "Somebody Killed Her Husband" in December, when she signed the contract. Before Poll allowed Farrah to sign anything, he had her give him "complete financial indemnity from any possible legal consequences." In plain English, that means it's Farrah who loses should the Spelling-Goldberg injunction be granted. The very threat of an injunction scared off Tom Miller and Ed Milkis, who wanted Farrah to star in their film, "Foul Play." They produce "Happy Days" and "Laverne and Shirley" for ABC and weren't about to throw themselves into jeopardy for anything.

As for ABC itself, they claim they haven't done a thing about getting studios not to hire Farrah, but they say they're behind Spelling-Goldberg, whatever they do. "The case goes far beyond the matter of Farrah Fawcett and 'Charlie's Angels,' " Fred Silverman, president of ABC Entertainment said. "It could establish a precedent about the manner in which business is done in Hollywood."

Farrah has not been sitting still. "Insiders" say her father's seven million dollar suit against ABC and "The Redd Foxx Show" for defamation of character (Redd did a skit in which everybody, down to the parrot, wore blonde wigs and was named Farrah) is her way of fighting back. It's still not settled.

Regardless of what anyone thinks the "real" reasons behind Farrah's departure are, not the least important of them has to do with her marriage to Lee Majors and keeping it solid and unshakable. David Doyle, her co-star on "Angels" explained what he thought was going on. "She's a sweet girl, and if she has a fault, it's that she thinks with her heart rather than her head.

"We all knew the problems Farrah was having. She is crazy about her husband and anxious to spend more time with him. But she would be up at 5:00 AM, work all day, and then get home at around 7:00 PM. Lee would get home from tossing buildings around about 7:30, just in time for a bite to eat. Then they would study their scripts and go to sleep. On weekends, Farrah was off shooting commercials. It wasn't any bed of roses."

David had as much to lose if "Angels" went off the air as anyone, but he could understand why

Farrah left. And he doesn't resent it; in fact, he thinks it was pretty silly to try and force Farrah to come back when she obviously didn't want to. The concept of the show was about three angels, and there are, still, three angels. The show is in the top three across the country, despite the absence of Ms. Fawcett-Majors. But, David says, and he speaks for the rest of the cast, "We all feel she made a terrible mistake leaving the show. One flop movie can put you out of action."

Obviously, Farrah didn't think it was a mistake, nor did Lee. He, though, did not have to quit his show, which would have closed up shop had he done so. The new schedule for "The Six Million Dollar Man" leaves him much more free time than before. They only shoot for about six months, so he'll be able to do his movies during the rest of the year. Farrah, meanwhile, is being selective about scripts. She is tired of roles that make her look "silly and giggly," but she is aware of the fact that she isn't exactly Academy Award caliber—at least not yet. "I'm certainly not a Faye Dunaway," she admits. "There are certain parts I cannot do, but I'm learning all the time."

The kinds of scripts she's looking for are not the heavy dramas like the ones Joan Crawford made in the 40's; or even the "new wave" feminist-type scenerios like "Julia" or "Mr. Goodbar." She'd like to play an earthy character, maybe a woman struggling for survival in the rough frontiers of the Old West. Farrah would like to be cast in challenging roles. Even when she was first starting out as an actress, Farrah was usually cast as an airline stewardess or a beauty contest winner. She never got the opportunity to play a troubled housewife or an ordinary salesgirl: she was much too beautiful to be believable in such mundane roles, they told her. This is undoubtedly one of the problems she feels pretty girls have.

Most people don't realize that Farrah has a real comedic streak, and she'd love to get into something light and frothy: a romantic comedy about a warm and human relationship in the classic tradition of Gable and Lombard, or even Rock Hudson and Doris Day. It was never a burning ambition of Farrah's to be an actress, or anything else specifically, for that matter. She remembers asking her mother about what she wanted to be as a child, and Mrs. Fawcett told Farrah that, at age five, she had told her that she wanted to be a nun. And that's all she ever said about the subject.

Farrah Leni (pronounced Le-nay) Fawcett is an Aquarian, born February 2, 1947. Amazing as it may seem, that's her real name. Her mom, Polly, made it up to go with Fawcett, as she did with Leni, by putting different syllables together until she got just the right sounding combination to perfectly complement Fawcett (in college, her friends called her "Drippy," not because she was, but because of her last name; in the late summer of 1977, Farrah gave her endorsement to a miniature gold faucet charm to be worn on a necklace or a bracelet and to be marketed with her name. Naturally, Farrah's Faucet is turning out to be a gusher).

She almost didn't make it through the first month of life. Farrah was born with a tumor between her upper and lower stomach, and the operation to remove it was a delicate one, not guaranteed to succeed. It was a horrifying time for her parents, but they decided to go ahead with it. Her father, James, even had to help during the operation because of a shortage of nurses in the hospital. He remembers it as being "the hardest thing I ever had to do—to squeeze her head very hard to expose a vein so that they could give her plasma."

Farrah pulled through without complications, but it still amuses her mother to hear people call her perfect. "She has a scar from the operation," says Polly Fawcett, "so she isn't all perfect."

It's just good-natured jesting, the kind that marked Farrah's childhood and supplied the seeds for her own fine sense of humor—genuinely funny, never malicious. Her parents' values are the same ones Farrah believes in today, old-fashioned, understanding, encouraging, but religiously-oriented, and very definitely not permissive. Her dad was, and still is, a successful oil field contractor; her mom, a housewife. Farrah was expected to obey their rules, and she did. "I was never rebellious as a child," she says. "I listened to my parents, helped my mother with the dishes, and studied hard in school." She'll expect and demand no less from her own children.

Farrah was an honor student at St. Patrick's parochial school and W.B. Ray High School in Corpus Christi, Texas. She was friendly and outgoing, but never a show-off. She was concerned about others and always tried to bring a little ray of sunshine into everyone's life with her bright smile and pretty face. (Lee often calls her "my little ray of sunshine," and he means it.)

In high school, Farrah was voted the most beautiful girl in her class three years in a row, but she never let it go to her head. She wasn't much for the frantic dating and extravagant socializing scene. She preferred one steady boyfriend, and a small, close circle of friends. Even at the University of Texas, in Austin, there wasn't a male around who didn't chase after the beautiful blonde. But, batting her beautiful green eyes, she turned down several weekend invitations by insisting that her mother had to go along as chaperone. It didn't stop the boys from asking. Even if the invitations did taper off, the admiring glances never let up for a minute.

When Farrah arrived at Austin, it was to study microbiology, but it didn't take very long for her art courses to become more important to her than the science ones. She found she was good at painting and sculpture and loved getting involved in projects that meant working with her hands. She switched her major to art and stuck with it through her junior year. When she left school, it was because everyone else was leaving, her boyfriend was off to Europe, her girlfriends were getting married and moving all over the country, and the persistent calls from Hollywood finally wore down her resistance. As a freshman, Farrah had been voted one of the University's "10 Most Beautiful Co-

Eds," the first freshman to ever be included in that elite group. Part of the honor was having her picture sent to a group of Hollywood talent agents. They were impressed and starting calling, and calling, and calling. Farrah kept on saying no. She wasn't interested in the riches being offered. She simply wanted to stay in school and finish up her education. "I had never thought about a career as an actress," she remembers. "I wasn't even in drama class." She did do some modeling and some commercials for local merchants, but her art studies were the important thing. When she finally did give in and leave school, her father was truly disappointed. He had wanted her to graduate with straight A's, and she had been well on her way. He took away her credit cards, and Farrah was amazed to find with the credit cards went her credit. Her mother though urged her to go to Hollywood and "have a good time," and even drove her out there herself. She set Farrah up at the Hollywood Studio Club, an all-women's boarding house, leaving nothing about her daughter's social future to chance.

Farrah remembers her early days in Hollywood with fondness and wistfulness. "I had never been on a stage in my life, and I felt I didn't have the drive to become an actress. I came out to Hollywood assuming it would just be for the summer. Then everything started to happen fast."

She admits to about two weeks of tears and tantrums and thinking that Hollywood, agents, the whole thing, was not for her. Then she met Lee

Majors, who introduced her to his agent. "Before I knew it," Farrah recalls, "Screen Gems was offering me a contract at $350.00 a week. In addition they offered to give me acting lessons, horseback riding lessons, etc. I said to myself, 'This is terrific. I'll go back home when I feel like it.' " It wasn't until she married Lee that she stopped thinking of Corpus Christi as home. After all, she hadn't come to Tinseltown to be a star. It just sort of happened that way.

Farrah was such a young innocent at that point that when she got her first W-2 forms in the mail, she didn't know what they were, so she tore them up and tossed them out. Her father came to the rescue and explained the complicated pieces of paper to her and what she had to do with them; she wasn't even aware that she was supposed to pay taxes.

The first commercial Farrah made that got on the air was for Ultra-Brite toothpaste. Her dazzling, almost blinding smile sparkled on TV screens across the nation, and millions of women not only envied her perfect teeth, but her tawny beauty and athletic figure. She was a perfect salesperson—it's easy to see why a TV viewer might hope to look as fabulous as Farrah just by using toothpaste, or any of the 100 plus products she has pushed over the years. She is probably best known for her Wella Balsam and Mercury Cougar ads, but she was also the gorgeous blonde who upstaged Joe Namath for Noxema. She is the quintessential all-American beauty selling everything from soda pop to sunglasses. She was in such demand she asked for—and got—as much as $30,000 a *day* for her services.

Her acting career, however, was growing less spectacularly at this point. For her bit part in Claude LeLouche's "Love Is A Funny Thing" she got close to scale. And for her small role in "Myra Breckinridge," they added a lot of grief. Raquel Welch didn't appreciate a rival beauty on the set; Mae West was furious because she had been promised that she would be the only blonde bombshell in the movie.

But for Farrah, despite the clash of egos, "Myra" was a learning experience. And what she learned was that she didn't ever want to have anything to do with a project on which she wasn't having a good time and getting paid a lot of money. And because of all those lucrative commercials, she could afford to be choosy. So she selected TV movies like, "The Feminist and the Fuzz" and "Murder on Flight 502"; guest appearances with Lee on his two series, "Owen Marshall, Counsellor At Law" and "The Six Million Dollar Man"; a running spot on "Harry O," with David Janssen; another movie, "Logan's Run."

When she was offered the role on "Charlie's Angels," she wasn't sure she wanted to accept. She liked the general idea of the show that someone was finally letting pretty girls "do more than just walk through the background," and from the beginning she never thought that the show was sexist or exploitive; in fact, she was totally happy with it.

"First of all, I'm a woman," she says, "and any woman who says she doesn't use her femininity to get what she wants is deceiving herself. Men don't have our instinct, and we don't have their strength."

So much for Farrah and Women's Lib. It's not that she doesn't believe in it—she'd just much rather do things for her husband to keep him happy and home. She gets upset at all the gossip that pops up about the state of her marriage, but Farrah's not exactly a stranger to malicious rumors. "It's been like that ever since high school," she sighs. "Some jealous girl would say she'd seen me kissing someone in a car—at a time when I was home studying. That sort of thing used to upset my parents terribly, but all I could do was ignore it.

"That's all I can do now. It's high school time in Hollywood. . . . How do I deal with it? I don't care about it for myself, but I worry about my parents and Lee."

Lee is, sometimes, something to worry about. Not that there's any danger of his leaving, but he does have very definite ideas of what he thinks a wife should be and how she should behave. And, at least partially, those ideas are responsible for Farrah's departure from "The Angels."

First there was their famous first date in 1968. Lee saw one of Farrah's pictures and decided that he just had to meet that girl. So he left a message at her rooming house informing—not asking—her that he would be by at 7:30 to pick her up for dinner. Farrah was enraged. Texas girls are simply not accustomed to being treated that way, and she was angry at this man's presumptuousness. Why, they had never even met! Lee realized that perhaps he had been a bit brash and called to apologize. Farrah was won over and agreed to go out to dinner. "I remember melting into a thousand pieces when he picked me up," she says. "It was love at first sight, I guess." They spent the first ten minutes of their first date in total silence, except for Lee's muttering, "You're really beautiful," so under his breath that Farrah didn't even hear him. They went to a discotheque, where after one sip of her drink, Farrah disappeared into the ladies' room for half an hour.

Poor Lee. He didn't know what was happening. Was she sick, or did she hate being with him that much? It was just nerves, he later found out, but the very next morning Farrah found a bouquet of 13 yellow roses outside her door. It was only the first of many Lee sent in their ten years together. They were seriously dating until July 28, 1973, when, in an old-fashioned and wonderfully romantic style, they were married. There were swans and soft music, quotations from Kahil Gibran, and Farrah in fairy tale white, with a handsome, smiling Lee by her side.

It was Lee, however, who insisted on the unique 6:00 PM cutoff in her "Charlie's Angels" contract so she could get home in time to cook his dinner. She's not superhuman, she says, she just loves to cook, and loves Lee. The Majors do have a housekeeper and a houseboy for the more mundane things, like marketing and cleaning.

"I like my marriage and his being the most important thing in my life," Farrah says. She feels a responsibility to Lee and the vows they made at their wedding, and can't imagine ever feeling differently. But it was difficult to maintain a house and a marriage when you had to get ready to leave for work at 5:30 AM. For Farrah, it usually meant getting up 1 ½ hours before Lee to do a little cleaning up, get his breakfast ready, and get herself ready. And evenings meant not just dinner but a good scrubbing to get off all that make up, studying lines, and preparing for the next day. Often the Majors would eat dinner in their cozy French provincial bedroom with a roaring fire in the fireplace, and konk out early. Weekends, when Farrah wasn't shooting for Max Factor, or some other client, they spent their precious hours at the beach, playing tennis, or just talking to each other—telling each other how glad they were to finally be alone.

Lee at one time thought it might be nice to have Farrah on the set with him every day while he shot "The Six Million Dollar Man,"—sort of to keep his eye on her. Farrah didn't see it that way. . . no marriage could last under those exacting circumstances. "Men often think they know what's best, but it's women who really understand," Farrah says. "What Lee really wanted, though he didn't realize it, was mystery. Was I going to be there on time? What was I doing on any particular day? That makes a relationship work. The mystery."

It keeps a marriage lively and always exciting. Farrah is not the type of woman who would be happy with a man who "yes darling, whatever you say" 'd her to death. She needs a little healthy argument every now and then to clear the air. As Lee puts it, "We fight as hard as we love, and we love as hard as we fight." They don't always agree with each other about their work or their lives, but then, what couple does? They give each other great latitude and freedom, which makes their time together so much more important. As for the rumored jealousy Lee has been harboring because of his wife's gorgeous, famous face, he laughs at it all, happy for her, and happy to think that maybe he helped a little. Sure he'd like Farrah by his side 24 hours a day. Who wouldn't? But he'd also sit back and let her support him if that's the way things happened to turn out. "If something happens to my career," Lee says. "I'll just devote all my time to being Mr. Farrah Fawcett. It's not what I expect, but it's also not so bad."

For the moment, Lee doesn't have to worry. Even though the ratings on his show are no longer in the bionic category, he's not in much danger of having to give up his cybernetic limbs. And he has other irons in the fire. More movies for TV; his own productions.

Farrah, meanwhile, is doing all she can to keep her face familiar and her name on the lips of her millions of fans. She's a strong lady, not one to be pushed around, and she has managed, so far, to stay right on top of the popularity polls. She has been described as "natural," "breathtaking," and "lovely," and her hairdo has been the envy of thousands of women who have rushed to their hairdressers demanding to be Farrah-ized. The Farrah tresses are her trademark, along with her sparkling smile, and she'd probably be a lot less recognized without them. Before "Angels," her long, luxurious blonde hair was worn in a simple flip. Surprisingly, according to Wella, Farrah did a fabulous job for them with women between 25-30 because of her own maturity. She helped increase sales by almost 15 percent. But Wella wants more —not only a 20 percent rise this year, but the younger market. So they replaced Farrah with her replacement, Cheryl Ladd. Wella hopes she'll convince teenagers to wash and condition their hair the Wella way. They feel that in a year, "more people will know more of Cheryl than of Farrah."

Cheryl says it would be a lie not to admit it didn't bother her to always be compared to Farrah. "But," Cheryl says, "we're entirely different people. I am also a singer. I perform with a band. And I have a lot of talent to offer."

Farrah hasn't seemed to mind. She's happily Fabergé-ing herself all over TV and magazines, and it's rather unlikely that anyone will forget who she is. She said of the show's new season and her replacement, "I never bother to watch it. I don't consider Cheryl a replacement at all—she hasn't got a great deal of talent."

Students of popular culture around the country have explained the Farrah phenomenon in terms of her looks. She is seductive but safe, "a cross between a Madonna and a Delilah," as one professor put it, unlike Marilyn Monroe (to whom she's forever being compared) who had a vulnerability along with her smouldering sensuality that made you want to reach out and comfort her. Farrah is cool, fun, the kind of girl you'd like to take home to mother. Innocent, but with a sort of wild abandon.

Her hair is very alluring to men. It's slightly messy, even though it's carefully styled; a sort of carefree, windblown, outdoorsy look that's exciting and appealing. Long, flowing hair has always been one of the ultimate symbols of femininity—look at Lady Godiva or Rapunzel; without their cascading tresses, where would they be? And where would Farrah be?

The combination of her femininity and her athletic and aggressive physique is also exciting. She is a beautiful female with a career that is not a threat to men, and is admirable to women for two reasons: one, because she is fulfilled, professionally and personally; and two, because she is married to a man who is an attractive, masculine figure in his own right. Farrah manages to have the best of both possible worlds, and there's no question that "Charlie's Angels" played a big part in getting it for her. "I can't really put my finger on why the show is such a hit," Farrah said a few weeks into the first season. "I think maybe people are ready for glamour on TV. Women like watching women. The chemistry between us works."

Farrah also echoed Jaclyn Smith and Kate Jackson in saying that the three of them got along famously. Maybe they'd never take a vacation together, but they supported each other completely. No wonder Kate and Jackie were upset when Farrah left and were concerned for her future. They seem to have come to terms with it, and Cheryl Ladd seems always to have been there.

If Farrah was at all sad to leave the Angels, she preferred to keep it to herself. She's a naturally happy soul, even-tempered, who's basic philosophy is that whatever's going to happen, will happen. It's all been pre-ordained, and she has no control over it. So when she took a chance and left the show, even knowing that as a real actress she hadn't even begun to prove herself, it was with her usual, good-natured optimism. "I'm always up," she says. "Sometimes I have to say to Lee, 'You're a big grumphead.' But I need the strength in him, and I realize how lucky we are."

Even without Lee's strength, she'd make it. Farrah is a survivor, despite her wide-eyed innocence, and she knows not only her capabilities and limitations but that TV and film makers are much more interested in ratings and box office receipts than anything else. She's shy, but she's pretty fearless about making her own decisions. The only things she's afraid of are spending more money than she has (a rather groundless concern) and people following her in cars. But her judgment is usually sound. "I'm the only one who knows what I'm truly worth," she says firmly, "and at this point in my life, I'm not going to compromise."

All things considered, she shouldn't have to. She has a movie in the works, and when she arrived in New York City to film she was guarded by four strapping stuntmen to protect her from the crowds that were thronging the Regency Hotel to see their superheroine. (The only thing they got to see was the separate truck that brought her clothes from the airport to the hotel.) She has a husband who adores her and stands behind her every decision and another talent—sculpting—that she can turn to if she ever decides to give up acting. She has sold several pieces, although now Lee is the sole collector of her works, and she'd like to be able to give it more time. She'd like to have children, too, but until she's ready to devote a lot of time to them a family will have to wait.

Farrah likes and enjoys her life and will be happy whichever way it goes. Her dreams, she says, "are all being taken care of. I believe that if a person is born and they are exceptionally blessed, they have at one time or another paid their dues.

"And I have a feeling that in this life, at this time for me, everything's being taken care of for me. God has been very good to me, and I've been very blessed."

TV's Super Women

You've met them all, TV's prettiest and sharpest females; seven beautiful women who have changed the viewing habits of the world in just a few short television years.

They are separate and distinct personalities who, surprisingly, have a lot in common besides their superstar status. They've loved, laughed, struggled, cried, and worked hard to get where they are, and they all love being there. They've shared the pleasures and pains of fame and success, and they've come through it stronger, wiser, and happier—hoping that their own individual stars will shine on well into the future.